L COOK

Inside the
Earth

Alan Davis

Macdonald/Educational

Managing Editor Chris Milsome
Editor Chester Fisher
Editorial Assistant Anne Furniss
Picture Research Penny Warn
                       Jacky Newton
Production Stephen Pawley
Design and Research Sarah Tyzack
Educational Consultant Tim Bahaire
Series devised by Peter Usborne

First published 1972
Macdonald and Co (Publishers) Limited
St. Giles House, 49-50 Poland Street,
London, W1A 2LG

contents

SBN 356 03983 8

The underworld gods and monsters

Poseidon, the earthshaker

Left: The Ancient Greeks cast many of their gods in the role of animals, the particular animal being chosen to fit the character of the god. Poseidon, god of oceans and creator of earthquakes, was often represented as a black bull. *Right:* Some of the Hindu legends said that the earth stood on a golden plate supported on the backs of elephants whose shifting about was the cause of earthquakes. The elephants themselves stood upon a giant turtle representing the water-god Vishnu.

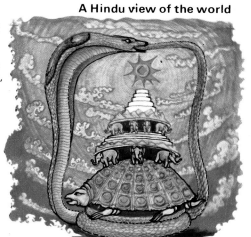

A Hindu view of the world

Myth and legend

For thousands of years man's life was governed by two powerful forces—Curiosity and Fear. His curiosity made him explore the land and wonder about the nature of his world. His fear of the unknown led him to invent explanations for everything he could not understand.

The ancient peoples of the world knew nothing of geology, physics or astronomy. To them the wind and rain, volcanoes and earthquakes, the great oceans and the stars became the Realms of the Gods. Throughout the world myths and legends developed, sometimes growing into complex religions.

The Yoruba people of Nigeria believed the primitive earth was covered in marshland until the Supreme Being, Ol-orun, sent the god Orisha Nla down from heaven to create dry land. The legends of Polynesia tell of the god Tangora who pulled the earth from the Great Waters whilst fishing.

Gods of the underworld

The legends of many lands associate the subterranean regions with the spirits of the dead and the forces of evil. In Greek mythology the god Pluto reigned over a vast underworld kingdom of the dead and kept watch over the earth's store of mineral wealth. Of all the Greek gods one of the most feared was Hephaestus, blacksmith and armourer to the warlike gods. His forges lay deep inside the earth beneath volcanoes. The violence and destruction of volcanic eruptions were thought to be an expression of his anger.

The forces under our feet have always been mysterious and only recently have we begun to understand them.

Cerberus **Pluto**

Below: Scandinavian legends are full of tales of the Trolls, who according to legend must return to their caves by daybreak or be turned to stone by the rays of the sun. Dwarfs were also thought to live and work underground.

Above: Pluto, the Greek god of the underworld, guarded a vast subterranean land of the dead and, helped by his fierce three-headed dog Cerberus, kept guard over the earth's valuable gems and precious metals.

Troll **Dwarfs**

Above: The Greek philosopher-scientist Aristotle lived from 384–322 BC. He wrote on politics, logic and the sciences. He believed that the earth was made from Earth, Fire, Water and Air, the "Four Elements", and that the stars and planets were fixed to spheres which enclosed the earth *(below).* Aristotle suggested that earthquakes and volcanoes were caused by winds trapped inside the earth. He observed an eruption on the island of Vulcano, which is north of Sicily. The heat of the volcano, he believed, was caused by the air becoming inflamed by the shock of the winds suddenly escaping from the hole in the earth. Many people disagreed with his ideas and thought that volcanoes were just burning mountains.

The classical scholars

In the period from 600 to 200 years BC Greek civilization produced some of the greatest philosophers of all time. They were among the first to seek logical explanations for natural events and are often called the Fathers of Science. Their methods were simple. Unlike modern scientists they had no previous experience on which to base their reasoning yet achieved remarkable insights into the nature of the earth, its size, shape and place in the universe. Eratosthenes' measurement of the earth's circumference stood unchallenged for 2,000 years. Euclid's original system of mathematics forms the basis of modern geometry.

The dark ages

The third century BC saw the rapid decline of Greek civilization. The rival city states were always at war. For many centuries wars of conquest raged across the Mediterranean lands and the whole of Europe entered the period known as the Dark Ages.

The growth of Christianity seemed to answer all questions. The Old Testament was accepted as a divine revelation and any who questioned it were condemned as heretics. For almost 1,500 years the search for knowledge was stifled throughout Europe.

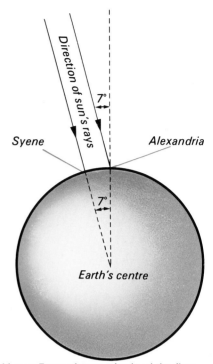

Above: Eratosthenes obtained the first measurement of the earth's size in the third century BC. He noticed that the sun was directly overhead at Syene in Egypt on Midsummer Day, but at the same time seven degrees from vertical at Alexandria. Because he believed that the earth was round and he knew that seven degrees was one-fiftieth of a circle, he was able to work out the earth's circumference. By multiplying the distance between the towns by 50, he got a good idea of the size of the earth.

Aristotle's view of the world

Earth
Water
Air
Fire
Planets
Signs of the Zodiac

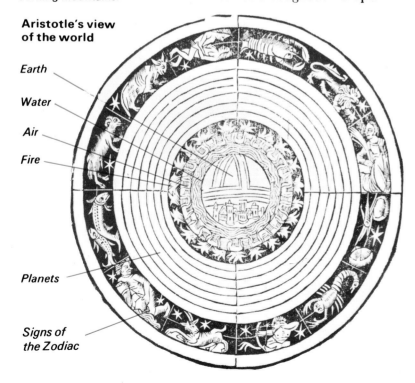

Above: The Greek philosopher Thales (624–545 BC) believed the earth was flat and floated on water. Adam and Eve are seen in this 16th century version of his ideas.

The Renaissance

In 14th century Italy a revival of interest in the arts and natural sciences heralded the end of the Dark Ages. The great voyages of Columbus (1492) and Magellan (1522) opened up vast new continents and finally proved the earth to be round. But the conflict between Church and Science persisted. Giordano Bruno was burned at the stake for teaching that the sun and not the earth was at the centre of the universe. It was many more years before scientists felt free to discuss their theories openly.

The emergence of a science

Throughout the late 18th century argument raged between the Neptunists who believed that all rocks had crystalized from one vast primitive ocean and the Plutonists who held that many rock types had been extruded from deep within the earth's crust. A young French geologist called Desmarest proved the Plutonists correct when he traced basalt lava flows across France to the original volcanic vent. The Industrial Revolution boosted geology by involving miners and engineers. By 1900 the young science was established and the stage set for the great advances of the 20th century.

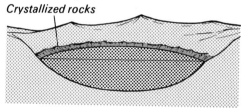

Crystallized rocks

Above: The Neptunists believed that all rocks had crystallized from an ancient ocean which had once covered all the earth many years ago.

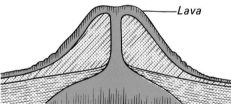

Lava

Above: The Plutonists believed that many types of rock originated deep within the earth and were thrown up by volcanoes. They did detailed research to prove this.

Above: The earth's interior as drawn by Athanasius Kircher in his book *Mundus Subterraneus* in 1665. Volcanoes were thought to be caused by great fires in the centre. *Left:* The rival theories of the Neptunists and the Plutonists. The Neptunists were named after the Roman god of the sea. They were led by a German geologist called Abraham Werner (1750–1817). The Plutonists, named after the god of the underworld, had the correct solution and began modern geology.

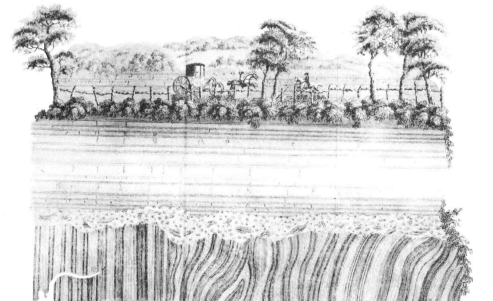

Above: James Hutton (1726–97) is widely regarded as the founder of modern geology. He first put forward the view that "the past history of the earth must be explained by what can be seen to be happening now". *Left:* An engraving from Hutton's *Theory of the Earth* of 1795.

The anatomy of the earth

Olivine

Above: Olivine. The inside of the earth is believed to be made up mainly of this mineral. Olivine is a mixture of iron, magnesium, silicon and oxygen. It is found in the crust wherever deep-lying rocks have forced their way to the surface.

Below: The diagram illustrates how the interior structure of the earth was discovered by the study of earthquake waves. Shock waves from the earthquake focus (where the earthquake starts) are felt at the epicentre, directly above the focus, and at all points on the surface round to 105° from the epicentre. All but a few P-waves then cease to be felt until 143° from the epicentre. This "shadow-zone" is caused by bending of the waves at the boundary of the dense liquid core. Extreme bending of a few P-waves by the very dense inner core causes them to emerge in the shadow zone.

X-ray by earthquake

The deepest holes yet drilled have no more than scratched the surface of our planet. Deep drilling programmes have revealed much information about the rocks of the earth's crust but a new approach was needed to unlock the secrets of the interior.

At the beginning of this century scientists discovered that earthquake waves consisted of two very different types of shock waves. Primary (P) waves could pass through both solid and liquid material. Secondary (S) waves could only pass through solids. The speeds of both P and S waves vary according to the depth and density of the rock they have penetrated. When passing through different kinds of rock both waves behave differently. Helped by sensitive instruments for measuring earthquake waves, a picture of the interior began to emerge. Studies of the waves revealed a dense liquid core which bent the P waves and absorbed the S waves. In 1936 a solid inner core was found by the same method.

Modern research has discovered that the earth has many layers at differing temperatures and pressures.

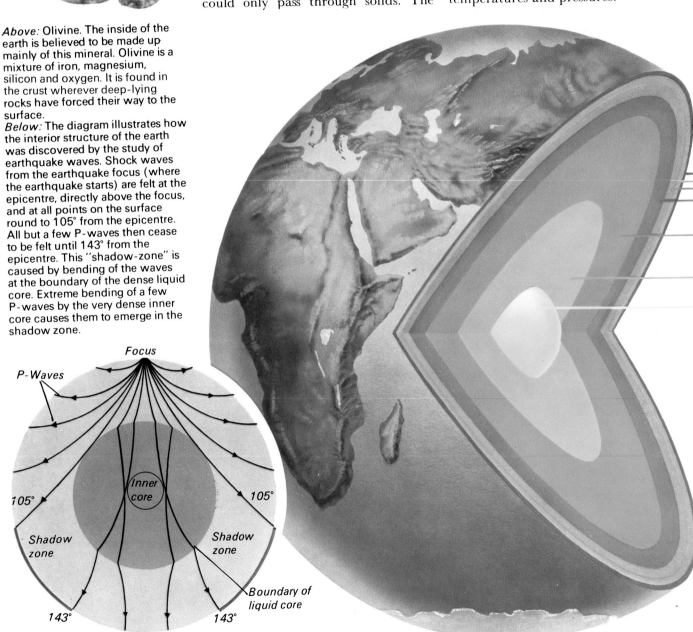

How earthquake waves reveal the interior

A gigantic magnet

Man has known that the earth is a gigantic magnet for over a thousand years. By stroking a needle with a magnetic mineral it is possible to find the Magnetic North Pole. Only recently have we begun to understand the earth's magnetism.

It is thought that there are electric currents deep within the liquid core of the earth. These currents are created when minerals of different temperatures and electrical properties come together. Electrical energy is therefore being created by a great generator within the earth. As all electric currents are surrounded by magnetic fields, this explains why the earth has a magnetic field. The rocks on the surface are also magnetized by this field and we have learnt much about the earth's past from this.

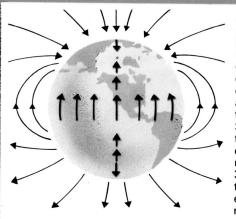

Left: Earth's magnetic field completely envelops the planet in an invisible forcefield focused on the magnetic poles. Although the overall field is roughly stable it does change in both strength and direction and travellers must always allow for magnetic variation when using a compass. Several times during the history of the earth the magnetic field has completely reversed itself. The most recent reversal was only 30,000 years ago—well within the history of man's existence on earth. It will almost certainly reverse itself again.

Right: Whenever new rocks form, small magnetic particles point the same way as the magnetic field of that time. These fossil indicators are held fast as the young rock hardens and, although some fading does occur, the magnetism may be detected after millions of years. In the diagram the underlying, and therefore older, rock shows a direction of magnetism very different from that of the younger, overlying rock.

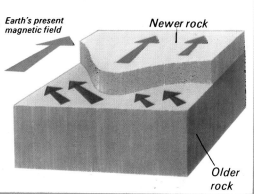

Earth's present magnetic field • Newer rock • Older rock

Surface plates
Plates of fairly dense mobile rock about 40 miles (64 km) thick on which float the continents.

Transition zone
Thicker than the surface layer, probably consisting of molten rock and semi-solid material.

Upper mantle
Dense rock in a solid state. Temperature around 2,000°C. Great pressure.

Transition zone
Largely composed of iron-magnesium silicates. It is between 250–500 miles (400–800 km) deep.

Lower mantle
Basically the same as the two overlying layers but increasingly dense. Temperature around 4,500°C.

Liquid core
Composed largely of iron and nickel. This zone is molten and in a highly mobile state.

Inner core
Composed of iron, nickel and some cobalt. Tremendous pressure keeps this region solid.

Below: A slice of the earth. This wedge taken out of the earth shows the scale and thickness of the major divisions. Pressure and temperature increase dramatically as depth from the surface increases.

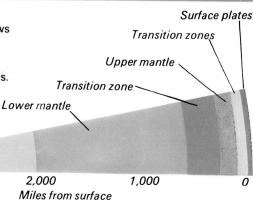

Surface plates • Transition zones • Upper mantle • Transition zone • Lower mantle • Liquid core • Inner core

Inner core — Liquid core — Lower mantle — Transition zone — Upper mantle — Transition zones — Surface plates

4,000   3,000   2,000   1,000   0
Miles from surface

Below: The minerals which make up the three major zones of the earth. Below the crust the proportions of the lighter minerals decline rapidly. The deep interior is almost entirely iron and nickel.

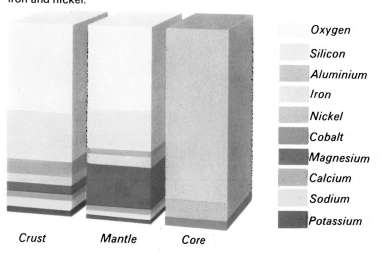

Oxygen
Silicon
Aluminium
Iron
Nickel
Cobalt
Magnesium
Calcium
Sodium
Potassium

Crust • *Mantle* • *Core*

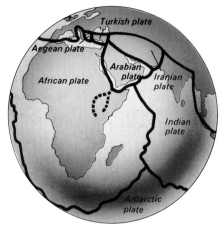

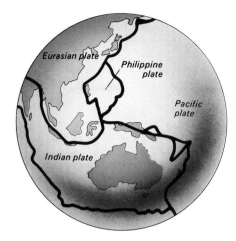

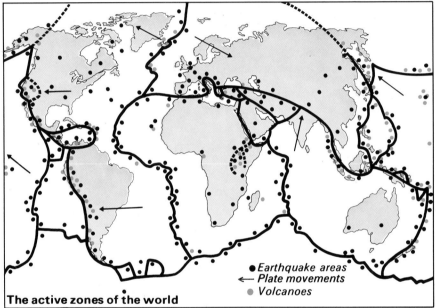

Earthquake areas
— Plate movements
Volcanoes

The active zones of the world

A revolutionary theory

The last 20 years have seen a revolution in the thinking of earth scientists. For many years scientists have been trying to find a theory to explain mountain building, earthquakes, volcanoes and the movement of continents. In the 1960s and 1970s a theory has rapidly developed which revolutionizes ideas about the earth. This theory is called *Plate tectonics*.

The surface of the earth is thought to be like the hard shell of a nut. The shell has been cracked in many places. The broken pieces are known as plates and are about 40 miles (64 km) thick. Instead of remaining still the plates are always moving around and jostling each other. At the edges of the plates many changes are taking place whilst their central regions remain stable.

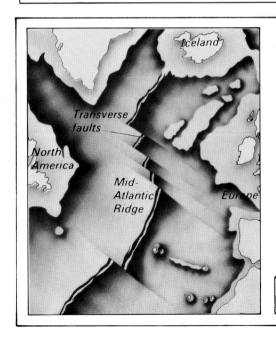

Left: The Mid-Atlantic Ridge is one of the most active areas of ocean bed growth. As the plates move apart (*below*) new basic rock wells up from below to fill the gap and, as the rock solidifies on the surface, it locks within itself a permanent record of the prevailing magnetic field. Over millions of years a record has been built up (*right*) of the changes in polarity of the earth's magnetic field.

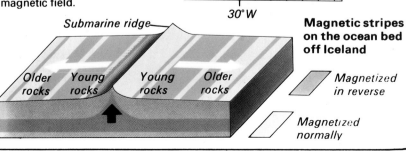

Ridge Crest

60°N

30°W

Magnetic stripes on the ocean bed off Iceland

Magnetized in reverse

Magnetized normally

Below and left: The plates which make up the outer shell of our planet are revealed in views of the globe. The plates themselves are rigid and all major geological activity, such as earthquakes and volcanoes, occurs along the edges of the plates.

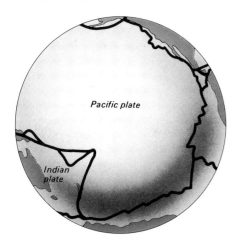

Pacific plate

Indian plate

Left: Lighter granite-like rocks of the continental "rafts" float partly embedded in the denser rocks of the crustal plate.
Below: Between the earth's crust and the mantle a sharp boundary has been discovered. It was discovered by a Croatian seismologist, Andrija Mohorovicic, and this boundary or discontinuity has been named after him. It is usually shortened to the *Moho.* It lies deeper under the continents than under the oceans.

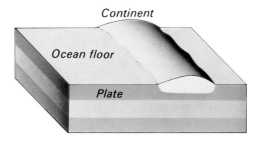

Continent

Ocean floor

Plate

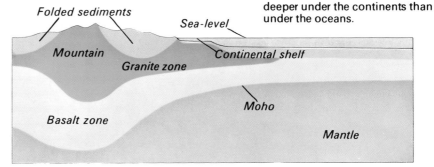

Folded sediments

Sea-level

Mountain

Granite zone

Continental shelf

Moho

Basalt zone

Mantle

Creation and destruction

Using the theory of plate tectonics we can begin to understand the workings of the earth's surface. If the positions of plates, earthquake regions and volcanoes are compared on a world map, a clear pattern can be seen. Earthquakes usually occur where two plates meet as in California or Japan. Most volcanoes are found along the edges of plates. In the oceans we find the ridges are sited along the plate margins. Large mountain ranges such as the Himalayas are also found near the plate edges. The pattern is clear, little activity is found in areas away from the plate margins.

Three types of plate movement have been found to account for this activity. The plates can be moving apart, allowing new rock to well up from the interior. Plates can be coming together, forcing one plate to dive under the other. The last case is where two plates are sliding past each other causing a fault as in California. All these movements take place over millions of years but we can see their effects today in the form of earthquakes and volcanoes.

Continents and oceans

The continents are made of very light rocks floating on top of the heavier rocks of the plates. As a plate moves the continent is carried along as a passenger.

The oldest rocks on earth are found in very stable areas of ancient continents, for example Greenland.

Oceans can be created or destroyed by plate movements. Plates moving apart will create new rock and force the sea-floor to spread. Where plates are moving together an ocean can be squeezed out of existence.

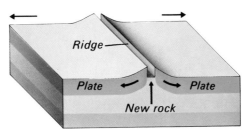

Ridge

Plate

Plate

New rock

Above: Ridges on the ocean floor are formed when two plates are moving away from each other. As they move away new rock wells up from the interior to fill the gap on the ocean floor.

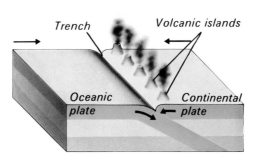

Trench

Volcanic islands

Oceanic plate

Continental plate

Above: Where a thin oceanic plate collides with a more stable continental plate, as happens off the coast of Japan, the oceanic plate is destroyed, forming a deep trench and a chain of off-shore volcanic islands.

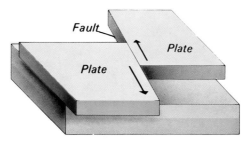

Fault

Plate

Plate

Above: Transverse faults are found throughout the length of the mid-ocean ridges and are probably due to differences in the speed at which different parts of the plate have moved away from the ridge.

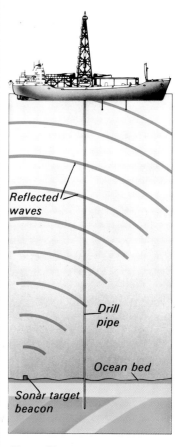

Reflected waves

Drill pipe

Ocean bed

Sonar target beacon

Above: The ocean research ship *Glomar Challenger* is designed to increase man's understanding of the earth's crust and the workings of plate movements. The ship is capable of drilling in water depths of up to 25,000 feet (7,620 metres) and is kept accurately in position by computer controlled positioning propellers. In order to keep the ship on station a number of sonar target beacons are placed on the ocean bed.

The earth in the past

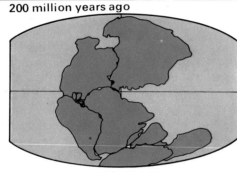

200 million years ago

The vast age of the earth

The earth is so old that the human mind can barely imagine it. From its fiery beginnings to the present day, the earth has been constantly changing. Only, now are we starting to get clues about the very ancient periods of the earth's history. The oldest rocks yet found, in Greenland, have been dated as 3,800 million years old. The first life on earth, single-celled organisms, are thought to have appeared about 3,000 million years ago. We know very little about the past of the earth until 600 million years ago, except that it existed. Careful study is now revealing the long and complex history of our planet.

Right: About 200 million years ago all the earth's land masses were grouped together in one vast super-continent called Pangaea. Shortly afterwards, at about 180 million years, Pangaea began to break up and to reorganize.
Above: At this time, the Triassic period, the dominant life-forms were the amphibians and rapidly developing reptiles. Insects were abundant and the first small primitive mammals had just appeared.

Below: A diagram representing the age of the earth. Each layer of the coil equals 600 million years. The top layer (blue) is the last 600 million years and shows the major events during that time. The coloured stripes are the mountain building periods and are keyed to the world map.

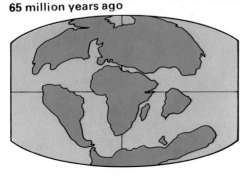

65 million years ago

Right: 65 million years ago, at the dawn of the Palaeolithic era, North America and Europe were still joined, but the gap was widening. India was well on the way to her collision with Asia.
Above: Animal evolution saw the rapid extinction of the ruling reptile class and the beginning of the rise to dominance of the mammals. Trees were the major plant form and true birds had developed from the reptiles.

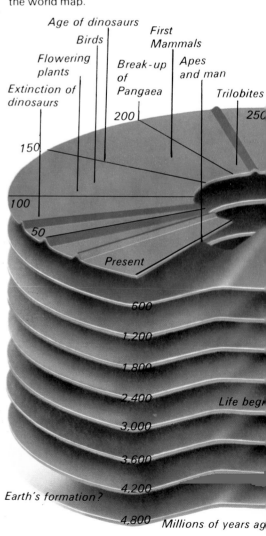

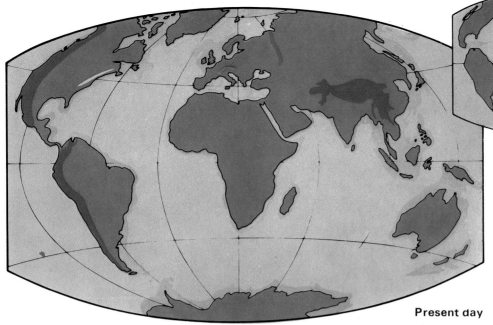

Present day

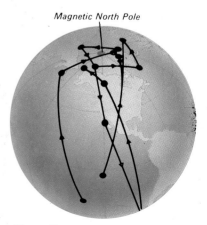

50 million years in the future

Left: The present day world map shows the major mountain formations. The continents now have their widest distribution since the break-up of the super-continent Pangaea, 200 million years ago. *Above:* In the future, trends which can be seen today will cause further changes. South America will become separated from the rest of the American continent. East Africa will be split along the Rift Valley and will begin to drift eastwards.

When the mountains of the world were built

- Himalayas
- Rockies and Ande
- Urals
- Alps
- Caledonian
- Appalachians

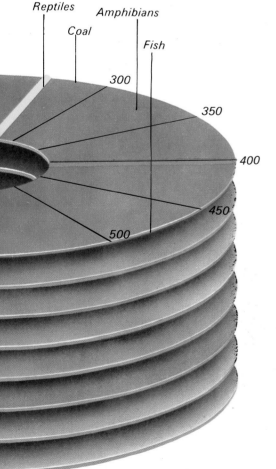

The age of the earth

Earth's changing face

Life on earth became abundant about 600 million years ago. From fossils we have learnt about the changing life, continents and mountains of the earth. Whole races of animals and plants have evolved, reigned and then vanished for ever. On the geological time scale man is the newest of newcomers.

The continents have moved around the earth. About 200 million years ago all the continents were clustered together in a vast super-continent known as Pangaea. Since then the continents have drifted apart and are still drifting. Coal seams found in the Antarctic indicate that it was once in a temperate climate. Most of the mountains in the world today are youngsters created in the last 100 million years. The surface of the earth must have changed many times since its formation.

How old is the earth?

Many rocks and minerals contain radioactive elements which are by their nature unstable. The atoms of these elements naturally decay into simpler, more stable atoms. By measuring the proportions of changed and unchanged atoms in a rock sample, a close estimate may be made of its age. This method has given an age of 3,800 million years for the oldest known crustal rocks.

However, the earth itself must be much older than the crust and to obtain an age for the planet we must measure the age of meteorites which formed at the same time as earth In this way scientists have estimated the age of the earth at 4,600 million years.

Above: Coal seams exposed in the impressive cliffs of the Theron Mountains in Antarctica bear witness to a past age when the continent had a temperate climate and extensive forest cover.

Magnetic North Pole

Above: Fossil magnetism held in ancient crustal rocks shows an apparent wandering of the magnetic poles. In fact the poles have remained in the same place and the continents themselves have moved over the earth's surface.

Mountain building where continents meet

Convection currents

The movement of plates over the surface of the earth must be powered by some great force. Rising and falling currents called *convection currents* are thought to provide this power. The currents operate beneath the plates and cause the formation of ocean ridges and mountains. Below are illustrations of how they might work.

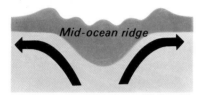

Above: The convection currents are pushing upwards and so pushing the plates apart. Rock then forces its way up to form an ocean ridge.

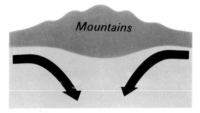

Above: The currents are going down and so forcing the plates together. When the plates meet they can force up mountains like the Himalayas.

Below: The block diagram illustrates the major types of folding and faulting caused by pressures in the rocks of the earth's crust.

The formation of fold mountains

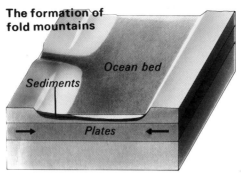

Above: 1. Carried along by convection currents deep within the earth the crustal plates move towards each other, gradually squeezing the ocean bed sediments upward.

Colliding continents

The mountains of the world have had a violent history. They are the spectacular evidence of the tremendous forces at work within the earth. Mountains were once flat layers of rock between continents. The movement of the plates which form the surface of the earth forced them up into mountains. A slice through any mountain range would show how these layers have been folded, broken and buckled into their present formations. The moving around of the continents over millions of years has led to collisions. Where the continents collided there was an impact which pushed up rock layers into mountains. The continents are still moving so we must expect new mountain ranges to be formed in the future.

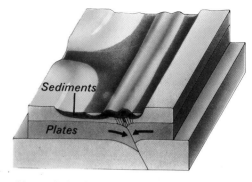

Above: 2. As the plate margins meet, the oceanic sediments begin to buckle under the great forces and one of the plates is pushed down into the crust.

Folding and faulting

The plates on which the continents stand must be moved by some force. It is thought that within the earth there are currents of heat which rise and descend. These *convection currents* push the plates along and thus cause the collisions and mountain building. The different types of mountains are therefore caused by these currents. Where the currents pull the plates apart, large blocks of land are likely to drop and form a rift valley with steep sides. If the currents are pushing upwards they may form block mountains with steep slopes and plateau tops.

Plates which are being pushed forward by convection currents will force rocks to bend over and form fold mountains like the Himalayas.

Types of folding and faulting

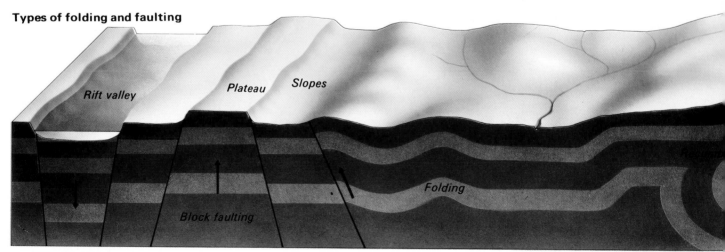

Above: Where the rocks of the crust are stretched or pulled apart by convection currents from inside the earth, downward block faulting occurs. Steep sided Rift valleys may also develop as in East Africa.

Above: In regions of large block faulting such as in East Africa, the Kalahari and in Utah, US, the mountains are made up of very steep outward facing slopes and flat or slightly inclined plateau tops.

Above: Gentle folding of rock strata with no associated faulting may be the result of slight local forces of compression or a major mountain building movement hundreds of miles away.

Right: Mount Everest towers over 29,000 feet (8,840 metres) above sea level in the Himalayas. Near its summit there are sedimentary rocks and fossils of sea creatures formed in a long-vanished ocean.

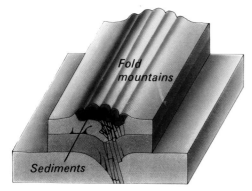

Above: 3. The ocean region has been destroyed. The sediments now form part of the fold belt which is forced up over the edge of the descending plate margin.

Where next?

The mountains of the world are clues to the past arrangements of the continents. Some 50 million years ago India collided with Asia to form the Himalayas. Italy was rammed into Europe, forcing up the Alps. The Americas drifted westwards as the Atlantic opened up, and the Andes and Rockies reared high as the American landmass overran the Pacific floor.

The geological processes which formed the Alps are still at work today. Very slowly the great raft of Africa is moving north towards Europe, squeezing out two small plates carrying Greece and Turkey. Some time in the future the Mediterranean will be engulfed and in its place will rise yet another range of mountains.

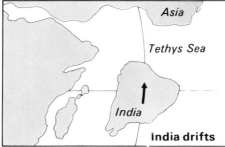

India drifts

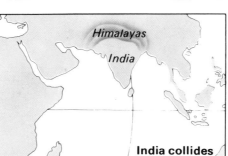

India collides

Left: After the break-up of the ancient super-continent Pangaea, about 180 million years ago, India was carried northwards across the Tethys Sea. It collided with the coast of southern Asia. The result of this collision was the Himalayas. All big mountain ranges were created by these continental movements and future ranges of mountains will also be formed in this way.

Below: The two photographs illustrate the two major forms of rock deformation, folding and faulting. The upper photograph shows a "normal" fault in which the rock, under pressure, has fractured so that one side has moved down and away (to the right of the photograph). The lower photograph shows rocks which have been folded right over to the point of breaking. This type of fold is called an over-thrust.

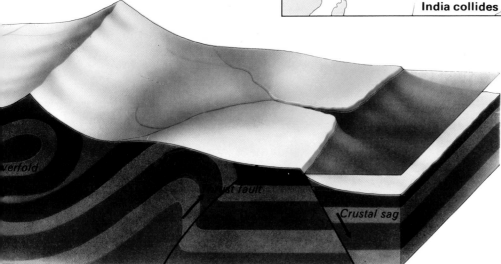

Faulted rock

Folded rock

Above: In a region of strong compressional forces the rocks are tightly folded and may even be forced right over into recumbent overfolds. If further pressure is applied the rocks may break along a thrust fault.

Above: Off the edges of the continents the enormous volumes of sediment carried from the land by rivers build up to vast thickness. The weight of these sediments may cause the crust to sag.

Rock formation the endless cycle

Obsidian
This is also known as volcanic glass because it is a super-cooled liquid. It is black or very dark green with shell-like marks on broken surfaces. Forms by the very rapid cooling of magma.

Basalt
Very heavy, dark basic rock made of basic plagioclase, pyroxene and olivine. The most abundant of the extrusive rocks (lavas). Lava flows often cool in the form of six-sided columns.

Granite
A hard, fine grained acidic rock made up mainly of quartz plagioclase, potash-feldspar and brown flakes of biotite mica. Often occurs as massive intrusions such as those forming Dartmoor.

Pegmatite
This is rather like granite but very coarsely grained. Formed from mineral-rich fluids cooling within a granitic mass. Pegmatite crystals can grow to be many feet in length.

How rocks are formed and where they can be found

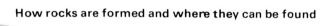

Slate
This is a fine-grained mud-stone or siltstone which has been physically and chemi-cally altered by heat and pressure. Hard and brittle, it can be easily split into thin sheets.

Granite gneiss
Heat and pressure has changed granite, an igneous rock, into this metamorphic rock. It is a coarse-textured rock with bands of various minerals such as mica and hornblende.

Conglomerate
A very coarse sedimentary rock made up of pebbles and gravel cemented together by silica, calcium carbonate or iron compounds. Often found on the sites of old river beds, lakes or coastal regions.

Oolitic limestone
A purely chemical limestone formed in warm, shallow seas or lagoons by precipitation of calcium carbonate onto tiny nuclei. Millions of round pellets are formed which are later cemented together.

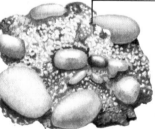
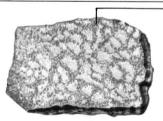

The rock families

The rocks of the earth are linked together in a great cycle of change. Rocks are always being formed, destroyed and again transformed into new rocks. Molten rock (magma) begins the cycle when it is thrown up from inside the earth by volcanoes. When magma hardens it forms the first of the three basic kinds of rock—*igneous* rock. There are two types of igneous rock—*extrusive* and *intrusive*. Extrusive rocks such as obsidian and basalt cool on the surface of the earth while intrusive rocks like granite and pegmatite cool underground.

The second family of rocks, *sedimentary*, is made up of fragments of rocks which have been deposited in seas, rivers and lakes. Rocks like limestone are formed on the sea floor from the remains of minute marine animals.

Inside the earth heat and pressure are always changing rocks into new types called *metamorphic* rock. The igneous rock granite can be transformed into a different rock called granite gneiss by heat and pressure. Sedimentary mudstone can be similarly changed into slate.

Above: The Grand Canyon. The Colorado River has cut through 10,000 feet (3,000 metres) of rock in about 21 million years to create the most impressive natural canyon in the world.

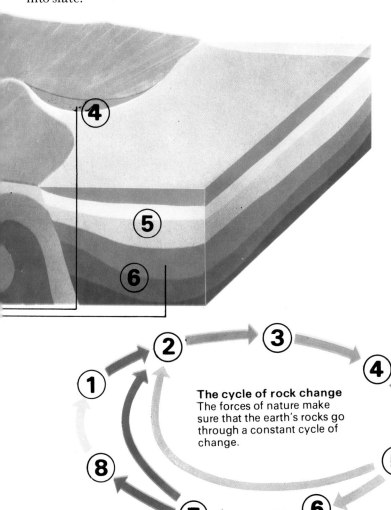

The cycle of rock change
The forces of nature make sure that the earth's rocks go through a constant cycle of change.

The processes of rock change

(1) Extrusion
New rock materials formed deep in the molten regions of the earth appear at the surface from volcanoes. They usually consist of lavas and ashes.

(2) Erosion
As soon as new rock is exposed at the surface it is attacked by wind, running water, glaciers and by chemicals in water, and worn down into small pieces

(3) Transportation
Rivers, glaciers and wind are also responsible for removing most of the broken-down rock debris from the land to the sea and lakes.

(4) Deposition
As soon as the river, glacier or wind begins to lose speed it also loses the power to carry its load and deposits it as sand or mud.

(5) Sedimentation
Deposits finally find their way to the sea floor where they build up to great thicknesses and cause the crust to sag because of their weight.

(6) Downwarping
A tremendous load of sediments is built up over millions of years. They are gradually dragged deep into the earth where they are remelted.

(7) Uplift
As one part of the earth's surface is worn down, other areas undergo readjustment and are lifted up.

(8) Intrusion
Many forms of igneous rock are forced up into the crustal rocks from below and only exposed at the surface when the rocks above them are worn away.

Earthquakes the violent earth

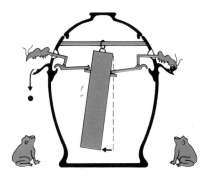

Above: This simple but effective earthquake indicator was developed in China around AD 150. When the instrument was shaken by an earthquake the suspended metal pillar swung across and caused a series of levers to dislodge one of the marker balls. The direction of the earthquake shock wave would be shown by where the dislodged ball fell.

Right: Finding out where an earthquake begins. The dots are earthquake recording stations. They can pick up earthquake shock waves and measure how far away they start. The epicentre of an earthquake is the point on the surface directly above the underground source of the earthquake. If the distance of the epicentre from a recording station is used as the radius of a circle it is possible to find the exact epicentre of an earthquake. The point where the circles of three different stations meet is the exact epicentre of the earthquake. Seismologists, people who study earthquakes, have estimated that about a million earthquakes happen every year throughout the world.

Earth's danger zones

Driven by convection currents deep in the mantle zone the plates of the earth's crust are in a state of constant change. It is at the plate margins that the earth is most active. As rocks are dragged down and destroyed beneath the continents new rocks are born again in volcanic mountain chains deep under the oceans. Enormous stresses build up as the masses of rock grind together and just as a stick will bend and then break, rocks will deform and then suddenly fracture, releasing their pent-up energy in the form of earthquakes.

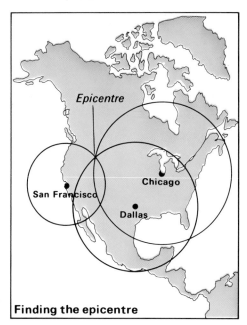

Epicentre

Chicago

San Francisco

Dallas

Finding the epicentre

Waves of destruction

Earthquake shock waves spread out in all directions, their speed varying with the type of rock. In dense rock such as granite the speed is far greater than in loose sand or gravel. The shock waves are strongest near the source of the earthquake and become weaker as they travel outwards. Even so, the shock waves from a major earthquake may travel right round the earth. When the volcanic island of Krakatoa exploded in 1883, the shocks were heard and felt over 3,000 miles away in Australia.

Every day dozens of earthquakes are registered by the world-wide network of *seismographic* stations. Fortunately most are weak but others have disastrous effects. In 1755 the city of Lisbon was totally destroyed by an earthquake equivalent to the explosion of a million tons of high explosive. Even greater destruction may be caused by tsunamis—gigantic waves caused by sudden movements of the ocean bed.

Taming the earthquake

Recent experiments in America may eventually show man how to control some types of earthquake. By locking the plates together at certain points, the energy might be released in a series of small "safe" jerks. This method, however, cannot control very deep earthquakes or those under the sea. The only way to combat the effects of these is to have a reliable forecasting system.

The history of an earthquake

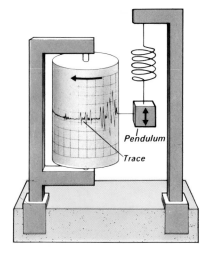

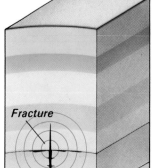

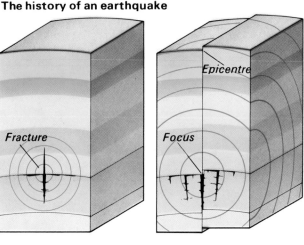

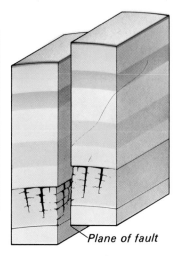

Pendulum

Trace

Above: A modern seismograph. The pendulum is made so heavy that it will remain still while the rest of the machine vibrates and makes a trace on the recording paper.

Fracture

Above: Rocks will bend under pressure until a point is reached at which they fracture, releasing an enormous amount of energy.

Focus

Above: Earthquake shock waves spread out from the origin, or focus. The epicentre is the point on the surface over the focus.

Epicentre

Plane of fault

Above: Once the rock has physically broken, the huge wedges of rock move past each other along a well-defined fault plane.

The plates round Japan

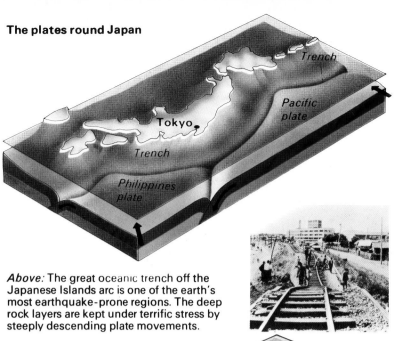

Above: The great oceanic trench off the Japanese Islands arc is one of the earth's most earthquake-prone regions. The deep rock layers are kept under terrific stress by steeply descending plate movements.

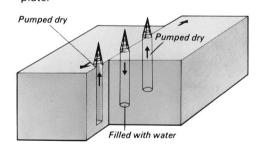

Left: The aftermath of a severe earthquake in Japan in 1964. The photograph shows the buckling of railway lines.

Above: The rapidly growing city of Tokyo is one of several major cities under constant threat of earthquake damage.

The San Andreas Fault

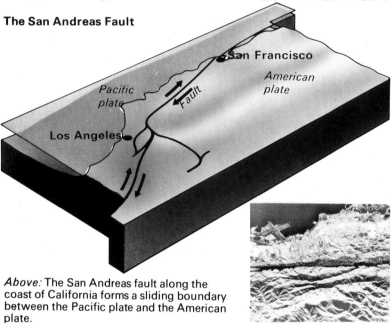

Above: The San Andreas fault along the coast of California forms a sliding boundary between the Pacific plate and the American plate.

Left: Seen from the air, the San Andreas fault, in California, stretches like a scar across the land for hundreds of miles.

Above: The City Hall of San Francisco after the disastrous earthquake of 1906 had devastated most of the city.

Above: Experimental work along the San Andreas fault suggests that shallow focus earthquakes may one day be controlled. The two outer boreholes would be pumped dry to "lock" the plate edges together by friction. Then water would be forced into the middle hole to lubricate the plates locally and cause a minor, "safe" earthquake which would not be able to extend past the locked areas. Though expensive, such operations would be vital if they could avoid the destruction of large cities such as San Francisco.

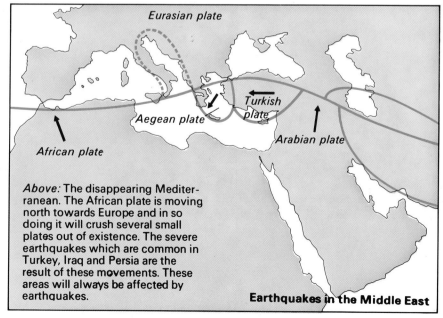

Above: The disappearing Mediterranean. The African plate is moving north towards Europe and in so doing it will crush several small plates out of existence. The severe earthquakes which are common in Turkey, Iraq and Persia are the result of these movements. These areas will always be affected by earthquakes.

Earthquakes in the Middle East

Fire from within volcanoes

Types of volcano

Above: The Vesuvian type. These have only one vent and may erupt with great violence blasting out glowing ash and lava.

Above: The Etnan type. Several vents lead off from the main chimney. Eruptions of gas and lava may burst from side vents.

Above: The Hawaiian type. A broad lake of very mobile lava is formed from which fountains of glowing spray are thrown.

Main vent

Lava flows

Layers of ash

Layers of lava

Dyke

Magma reservoir

Above: Rivers of molten rock pour dramatically down the sides of Mount Etna during a period of intense activity.

Above: Boiling hot water and steam are blasted high into the air by the Pink Dome geyser in Wyoming, US.

Earth's safety valves

Volcanoes are spectacular evidence of the intense heat and pressure within the earth. Molten rock called *magma* comes up from the interior and collects in reservoirs underneath the earth's crust. This magma is always trying to find a way to the surface. Where the crust is weak, usually along the edges of the plates, the tremendous forces exerted by the magma and its gases break a hole in the crust.

The type of volcano created depends on the material thrown out when it erupts. Some volcanoes explode with great violence when they break the crust while others just pour out lava. The typical volcanic cone, like Vesuvius, is formed by molten rock called *lava* cooling rapidly and combining with ashes. The cone is gradually built up into a mountain of layers of lava and ash. The Hawaiian type consists of a great lake of bubbling lava throwing out showers of glowing droplets. A third type—the *fissure eruption*—spreads out lava over vast areas from a long gash in the earth's surface.

Volcanic action is responsible for many formations inside the crust. The magma can find its way along narrow channels and harden to form *dykes* and *sills*. Magma hardening in a solid mass forms *laccoliths*. The heat of the earth is also responsible for *geysers* which throw out boiling water and steam at regular intervals.

The wearing down of a volcano

Stage 1: Layers of ash and lava are built up by successive eruptions of the volcano.

Stage 2: Erosion wears away the weaker parts of the volcano but the harder lava in the main vent remains.

Stage 3: After many years, the original vent is left standing as an isolated feature.

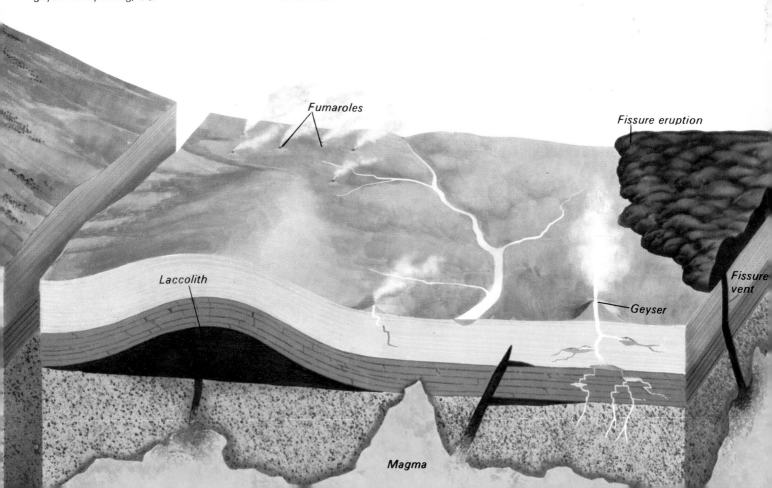
Fumaroles

Fissure eruption

Fissure vent

Laccolith

Geyser

Magma

Clues to the past fossils

The formation of fossils

Stage 1. A sea creature dies and falls to the seabed. The soft internal parts quickly decay and are washed away.

Stage 2. The empty shell is buried under accumulating sediments and very fine sediment begins to fill the cavity.

Stage 3. The shell material has dissolved leaving a mould. Sediment has filled the cavity forming a cast of the shell.

Mould   Cast

Stage 4. Millions of years later the hardened rock is broken open to reveal the cast and mould of the shell.

Above: The fossilized remains of an Ammonite shell. An Ammonite was a common sea creature in the Jurassic period.

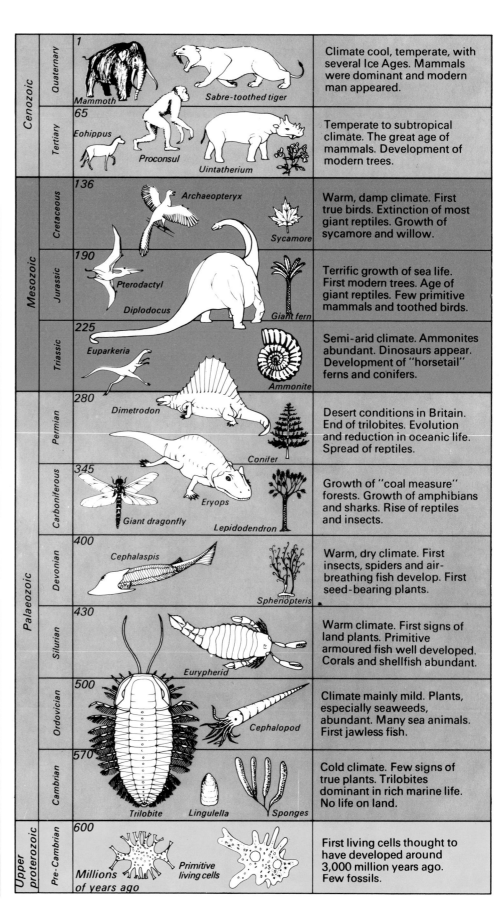

Cenozoic	Quaternary	1 — Mammoth, Sabre-toothed tiger	Climate cool, temperate, with several Ice Ages. Mammals were dominant and modern man appeared.
	Tertiary	65 — Eohippus, Proconsul, Uintatherium	Temperate to subtropical climate. The great age of mammals. Development of modern trees.
Mesozoic	Cretaceous	136 — Archaeopteryx, Sycamore	Warm, damp climate. First true birds. Extinction of most giant reptiles. Growth of sycamore and willow.
	Jurassic	190 — Pterodactyl, Diplodocus, Giant fern	Terrific growth of sea life. First modern trees. Age of giant reptiles. Few primitive mammals and toothed birds.
	Triassic	225 — Euparkeria, Ammonite	Semi-arid climate. Ammonites abundant. Dinosaurs appear. Development of "horsetail" ferns and conifers.
Palaeozoic	Permian	280 — Dimetrodon, Conifer	Desert conditions in Britain. End of trilobites. Evolution and reduction in oceanic life. Spread of reptiles.
	Carboniferous	345 — Giant dragonfly, Eryops, Lepidodendron	Growth of "coal measure" forests. Growth of amphibians and sharks. Rise of reptiles and insects.
	Devonian	400 — Cephalaspis, Sphenopteris	Warm, dry climate. First insects, spiders and air-breathing fish develop. First seed-bearing plants.
	Silurian	430 — Eurypherid	Warm climate. First signs of land plants. Primitive armoured fish well developed. Corals and shellfish abundant.
	Ordovician	500 — Cephalopod	Climate mainly mild. Plants, especially seaweeds, abundant. Many sea animals. First jawless fish.
	Cambrian	570 — Trilobite, Lingulella, Sponges	Cold climate. Few signs of true plants. Trilobites dominant in rich marine life. No life on land.
Upper proterozoic	Pre-Cambrian	600 — Primitive living cells. Millions of years ago	First living cells thought to have developed around 3,000 million years ago. Few fossils.

Life's record in the rocks

Fossils are the traces of animals and plants which lived on the earth in ages past. They form a permanent record of the remarkable succession of life on our planet.

The earliest fossils yet found are a few very simple algae about 2,700 million years old. The continuous fossil record, however, does not begin until the Cambrian period some 600 million years ago.

True vertebrates, animals with backbones, appeared in the Ordovician period (500 million years ago) and evolved very rapidly so that by the Devonian period (400 million years ago) sharks and armoured fish had appeared. The first amphibians also began to evolve. Throughout the 100 million years of the Jurassic and the Cretaceous periods, giant reptiles ruled the earth. About 70 million years ago the reptiles declined and were replaced by the mammals. Man is the latest addition to the mammal family.

We have learnt about the previous life on earth from the study of fossils. Greek philosopher-scientists, about 450 BC, recognized their significance but like much of their learning the knowledge was lost. Throughout the Dark Ages fossils were regarded as freaks of nature or even as the work of the devil.

The true nature and value of fossils remained a mystery until late in the 18th century. An English canal engineer, William Smith, realized that fossil types in one layer of rock differed from those in an adjacent layer. From his work grew the science of *palaeontology* which is one of the geologist's most useful tools in rock dating and identification.

Above: An ancient graveyard found in a cave in the United States. At Olduvai Gorge in Tanzania fossil bones of an ape-man have been dated as one and three-quarter million years old.
Right: An artist's reconstruction from bone fragments of an ape-man named Australopithecus. He is thought to have lived about one million years ago.
Below: A reconstructed skull of Australopithecus from remains found in South Africa.

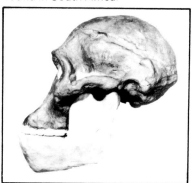

Australopithecus

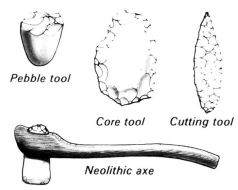

Pebble tool

Core tool   *Cutting tool*

Neolithic axe

Above: Tools used by ancient man. The pebble tool is over 500,000 years old. The core tool shows a better knowledge of tool manufacture. The cutting tool is a very efficient knife. The axe is a reconstruction of one found in Denmark.
Left: A cave painting done by prehistoric man on a wall in Altmira, Spain, where some of the finest examples of prehistoric art can be found.

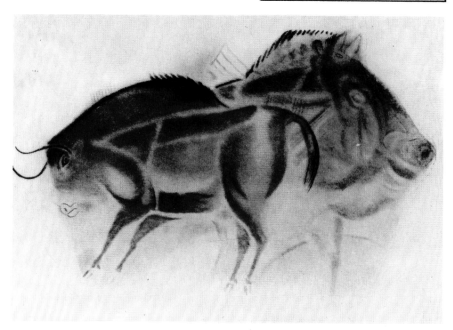

21

Underground exploration caves and caving

The underground world

In many parts of the world there are vast cave systems which are largely unexplored. The study of caves is called *speleology*. When a speleologist descends into the earth he enters another world. He is likely to discover enormous caverns, raging rivers and crystal-clear lakes. Exploring caves can be very dangerous as it is necessary to crawl through narrow passages, climb down sheer drops and to wade through streams. The efforts of the speleologists have enabled us to understand and see more of this dark and mysterious world.

Most caves form in limestone which is dissolved by slightly acidic rain-water. Other caves may be formed by the action of wind, waves and ice. Beneath the limestone country of Trieste lies the largest cavern in Europe, the Grotta dei Giganti. It is so large that St. Peter's in Rome would be dwarfed inside it. Under the Pyrenees, the Gouffre de la Pierre Saint-Martin plunges to a depth of 3,872 feet (1,180 metres), the deepest cave system explored. Many of the world's famous caves were found by accident. Today skilled exploration is revealing much more.

The formation of limestone caves

1. Slightly acidic rain water has started to dissolve carbonate rocks and create swallow holes.

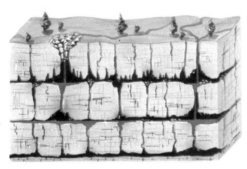

2. Swallow holes have become enlarged. Solution along lines of weakness creates the underground system of channels.

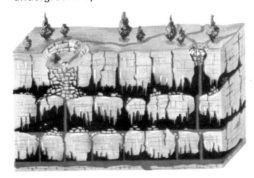

3. Full development of the cave system follows as roof falls and water erosion add to the effects of solution.

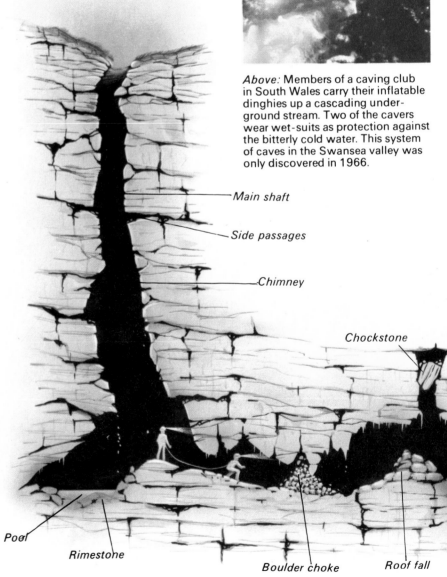

Above: Members of a caving club in South Wales carry their inflatable dinghies up a cascading underground stream. Two of the cavers wear wet-suits as protection against the bitterly cold water. This system of caves in the Swansea valley was only discovered in 1966.

— Main shaft

— Side passages

— Chimney

Chockstone

Pool

Rimestone

Boulder choke

Roof fall

A cave system showing typical features

A speleologist

- Lightweight helmet
- Nickel alkaline battery lamp
- Under pullover
- Boiler suit
- Nylon rope
- Whistle
- Diver's watch
- Karabiner
- Carbide acetylene torch
- Bag for camera, first aid and food, etc.
- Pocket for notebook, etc.
- Heavy duty boots

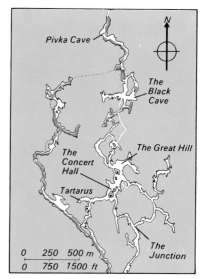

Above: The Carlsbad Caverns, New Mexico, which contain the largest cave in the world. As water drips constantly from the cave roof some of the dissolved carbonate is left behind on the rock face. Over millions of years this slow deposition can build stalactites and stalagmites of staggering beauty.

Left: The caver, or speleologist, must be fully equipped with stout boots, overalls, safety helmet, lamp and ropes before venturing underground. Even then the novice must be accompanied by someone with experience until he has learned the techniques of caving.

Right: A map of the Postojina caves in Yugoslavia. These famous caves extend for several miles and have many large chambers. Almost all the caves are open to visitors.

Pivka Cave

The Black Cave

The Great Hill

The Concert Hall

Tartarus

The Junction

| 0 | 250 | 500 m |
| 0 | 750 | 1500 ft |

Left: The large diagram shows some of the major features of a limestone cave system. The great vertical *chimney* is a feature of many famous caves but more commonly the cave descends in a series of short vertical *pitches* alternating with horizontal passages.

The base of the entrance *shaft* is always littered with rock debris, and the remains of plants and animals which have fallen into the shaft. Often this pile of debris, or *boulderchoke,* completely blocks some of the side passages.

A large boulder which becomes jammed in a narrow passage is known as a *chockstone* and is sometimes useful to the caver as ropes can be fastened to them.

Rimstone and *flowstone* are deposits formed by running water in the same way as *stalagmites* and *stalactites* and may coat walls and ledges wherever running water is present.

A feature familiar to any caver is the *syphon* or *trap* formed where the cave roof dips below the level of water in the cave.

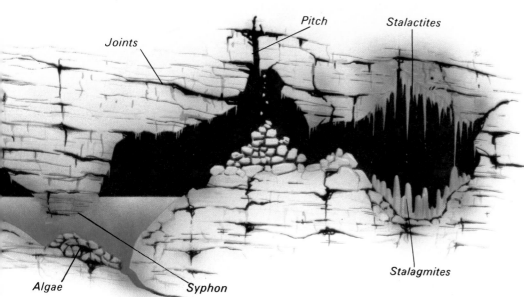

- Joints
- Pitch
- Stalactites
- Algae
- Syphon
- Stalagmites

23

Tunnelling roads through the earth

The need for tunnels

The earliest known tunnel was built by the Babylonians in about 2160 BC. It provided their king with a convenient route from his palace to a temple on the opposite bank of the River Euphrates.

Tunnels, however, were rare in the past. Transport was mainly by horse or foot and roads, if any, simply followed the lie of the land. The building of railways and canals in the 19th century, however, demanded completely flat land. To achieve this, tunnels had to be built through hills and mountains. The science of tunnelling was born.

Today, social and economic pressures demand a fast uninterrupted flow of road and rail traffic between big cities. This means expensive and complex tunnels such as the 22 mile (36 km.) Seikan railway tunnel in Japan.

As cities become more and more crowded the underground railway becomes ever more important. Without it cities like Paris, London and New York would grind to a halt, their streets unable to cope with the volume of traffic. Cities of the future may well be traffic-free as the car is replaced by fast underground railways.

A modern road tunnel

Fresh air inlet

Lights

Emergency footway

Drainage

Soft rock drilling machine

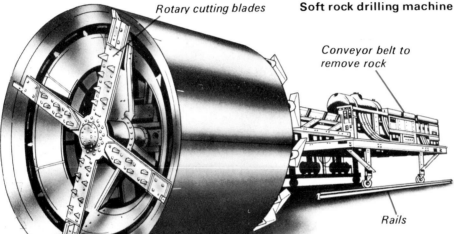

Rotary cutting blades

Conveyor belt to remove rock

Rails

Left: The four-metre diameter cutting face of this soft-rock tunnelling machine is driven by a powerful hydraulic motor. Such machines simplify the digging of tunnels in soft rock.

Building a tunnel in hard rock

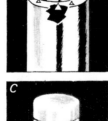

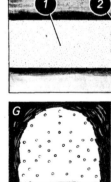

Before tunnelling can begin a detailed survey (A) must be carried out over the whole route. Test drillings are made to find the composition and strength of the sub-surface rocks and to check on the presence of water-holding strata.

A diamond tipped drill (B) is used to sample hard rocks whilst often a simple hollow tube may be forced into the ground to get samples of soft rock or soil. The core (C), showing different rock and soil strata, is sent to the laboratory for testing.

Where speed is essential it may be practical to sink vertical shafts and allow work to progress on several faces (D). Shot holes for explosives are drilled (E) using compressed air tools. The positions of the holes are carefully worked out.

Right: The opening of the Mont Cenis railway tunnel at Modane, Italy, in 1871.
Below: A cross-section of a modern road tunnel showing the main features of its structure.

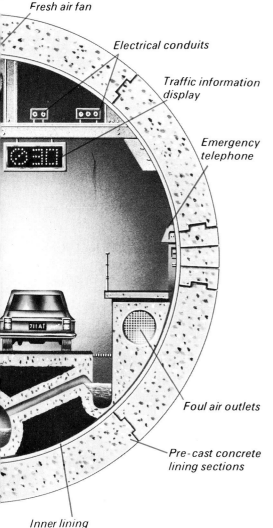

Fresh air fan

Electrical conduits

Traffic information display

Emergency telephone

Foul air outlets

Pre-cast concrete lining sections

Inner lining

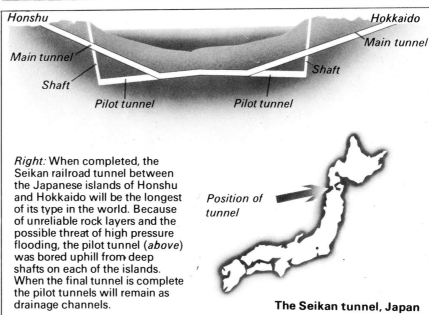

Honshu

Main tunnel

Shaft

Pilot tunnel

Hokkaido

Main tunnel

Shaft

Pilot tunnel

Right: When completed, the Seikan railroad tunnel between the Japanese islands of Honshu and Hokkaido will be the longest of its type in the world. Because of unreliable rock layers and the possible threat of high pressure flooding, the pilot tunnel (*above*) was bored uphill from deep shafts on each of the islands. When the final tunnel is complete the pilot tunnels will remain as drainage channels.

Position of tunnel

The Seikan tunnel, Japan

Diagrams (F) and (G) show a typical shot firing sequence. The charges nearest the centre detonate first, followed a second or two later by the others. The first blast creates a hole into which the debris of the later one can fall.

The tunnel is cleared of all workmen and equipment and the charge is fired by closing an electrical circuit (H). Parts of the charge: (1) Explosive, (2) Primer, (3) Gun-cotton, (4) Heat element, (5) Detonator, (6) Cables to battery.

After the blast (J) the smoke and dust are cleared by powerful fans, debris is removed by conveyor belt and taken away for dumping. Cast iron lining sections (K) are lifted into place by a hydraulic ram and are bolted together.

The mineral kingdom

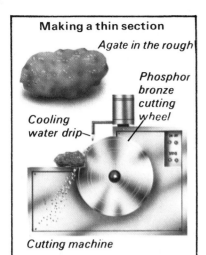

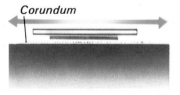
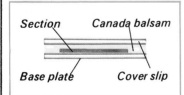
Colour and beauty

The rocks of the earth's crust are made up of many small components known as minerals. These in turn are built from basic chemical elements such as iron, copper, oxygen and sulphur. Some rocks consist largely of a single mineral. Chalk, for example, is almost pure calcium carbonate. Others, like granite and basalt, are built up from many different minerals.

The most common rock-forming minerals are the silicates and carbonates. Another group, the oxides, provide many important sources of mineral ores.

Examined under a geological microscope a thin slice of even the most dull-coloured rock may reveal an inside story of brilliant colour and beauty. The structure of the crystals and the chemical composition give each mineral characteristic properties from which it may be identified and studied.

Mineral crystals are normally microscopic in size but giant crystals may grow inside a large mass of slowly cooling molten rock. A single crystal of mica discovered in Canada measured 33 feet (10 metres) in length and weighed over 90 tons.

Granite

Garnet Schist

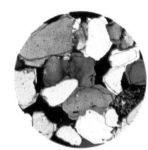

Desert Sandstone

A polarizing microscope

Above: The hidden world of colour. Viewed under polarized light these thin sections reveal the mineral colorations and aid the identification of minerals.

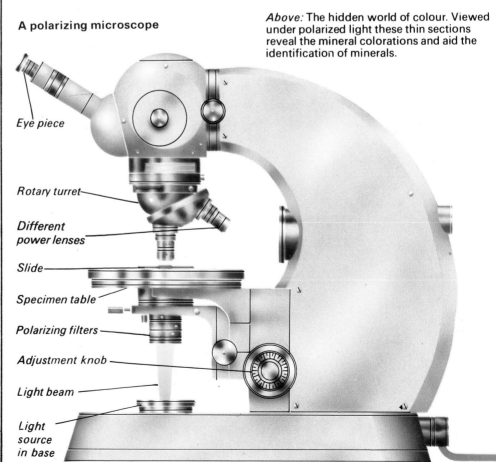

Eye piece

Rotary turret

Different power lenses

Slide

Specimen table

Polarizing filters

Adjustment knob

Light beam

Light source in base

The manufacture of synthetic gemstones

Because of their high value gemstones were amongst the very first minerals to be created artificially by man. In 1902 the French chemist August Verneuil succeeded in making a synthetic ruby. In his process, fine aluminium oxide powder is fed into a flame of hydrogen and oxygen gases at 3,750°C. This melts the powder and gradually builds up a pear-shaped *boule* of synthetic gemstone. The *boule* revolves on a turntable to give it an even shape. In 1910 the first synthetic sapphire was created and since then the number of artificial minerals has grown rapidly. Not only gemstones but also a wide variety of other minerals are made. Many synthetic minerals are used in the ceramics and electronics industries.

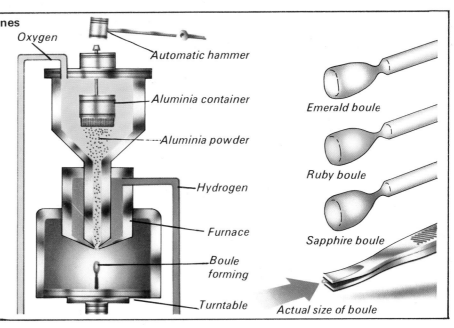

Oxygen
Automatic hammer
Aluminia container
Aluminia powder
Hydrogen
Furnace
Boule forming
Turntable

Emerald boule
Ruby boule
Sapphire boule
Actual size of boule

Pyrite

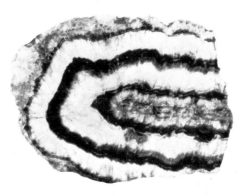

Blue John

Sulphur

Malachite

Azurite

Galena

Anglesite

Calcite

Prospecting the search for wealth

Above: In the 16th century hopeful prospectors tried to "sense" ore bodies with a forked stick. They believed that the stick would shake if a mineral was near.
Mid-19th century miners used the panning method to extract gold from river deposits. Water and gravel were swirled round in a shallow pan so that the gravel was washed over the sides but the heavy grains of gold remained in the pan. The rocking cradle *(right)* used in California was a development of the panning method.

The tell-tale clues

In the past mineral prospectors had to rely on surface evidence to indicate the presence of underground deposits. Oil-fields might be indicated by surface seepage or by the formation of lakes of tar or asphalt. Gold, silver and diamond prospectors had to spend months laboriously panning the gravel of river beds in the hope of finding tell-tale traces of minerals washed out of eroded rocks further upstream. Apart from these clues the wealth beneath the surface remained hidden until revealed by modern prospecting methods.

Modern x-ray methods

Twentieth century technology has given the modern prospector several methods of "seeing" into the earth's rocks as clearly as if they were transparent. The days of mule, pack-horse and pan are gone and the prospector today uses aircraft, electronic instruments and teams of trained technicians.

Modern prospecting methods rely on the physical properties of rocks, density and elasticity, and on electrical, magnetic and radio-active properties. The study of reflected shock waves will reveal underlying structures and provide information on buried rock types. Measurements of slight variations in the force of gravity may indicate the presence of dense deposits such as mineral ores or of light salt domes.

Magnetic rocks such as magnetite, one of the most important iron ores, may be "seen" by an airborne magnetometer flown thousands of feet above the earth's surface, and pitchblende is one of several radio-active minerals which give away their presence by the emission of charged particles.

Above: The gold rushes in America, South Africa and Australia saw thousands of people risk everything for the chance of finding wealth. The treks to the diggings were long and dangerous. So powerful was the 'gold fever' that people travelled for months by horse, cart, mule or even on foot carrying all their belongings.
Right: Photographs show some of the most important ores of precious metals and minerals.

Silver

Gold

Diamond

Modern prospecting methods

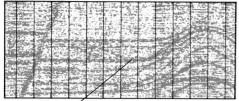

Seismic trace

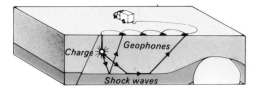

Charge · *Geophones* · *Shock waves*

Above: Seismic prospecting uses the man-made earthquake principle. An explosive charge is detonated below ground and the reflected shock waves are received by a series of detectors or geophones. The automatic trace or seismograph shows the geologist the underlying structure and rock type.

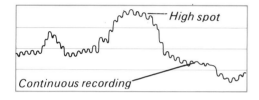

High spot

Continuous recording

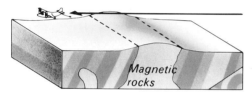

Magnetic rocks

Above: A sensitive instrument called a magnetometer may be towed behind an aircraft and set to give continuous readings of the strength of the earth's magnetic field. Wherever magnetic rocks occur beneath the surface they will show up as high spots on the continuous recording.

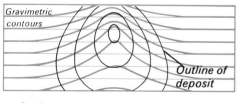

Gravimetric contours

Outline of deposit

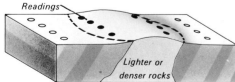

Readings

Lighter or denser rocks

Above: Gravimetric survey depends on the slight variations in the earth's gravity field caused by dense or light materials in the crustal rocks. Differences between the readings taken and the normal gravimetric contours (fine orange lines) are plotted on a base map. This may disclose the outline (black lines) of hidden light or dense materials.

Above: The photograph shows members of a geophysical prospecting team in Nigeria preparing a shot hole as part of a seismic survey. The shot hole may be drilled down as far as 200 feet (60 metres) before the dynamite charge is placed in position and fired by remote control. Reflected shock waves received at carefully positioned geophones (see above left) reveal the geology of the area and give an idea of the minerals underground.

Below: Over 3,520 feet (1,072 metres) deep, the famous "Big Hole" at Kimberley, South Africa, is the deepest open excavation ever dug by man. Due to rising costs work ceased in 1908, but there are plans to reopen it in the future. The shaft of the mine outlines the position of one of Africa's many diamond pipes—ancient volcanic vents blocked with rock known as kimberlite. Many minerals are found in the rocks, the most valuable being diamond.

The master metals iron and steel

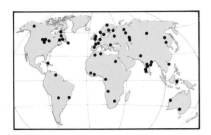

Above: The world map shows the major producers of iron ores.

Above: An iron foundry of the type common in 18th century England.

The long history of iron

Iron making has a long and complex history. Discovered almost certainly by accident, some 5,000 years ago, its use spread slowly from the Middle East through Europe and reached Germany about 900 BC. The early processes were crude, producing a pasty mass of impure metal which could be shaped by reheating and hammering. The open furnaces, or "bloomeries", of the Middle Ages were better but could not produce temperatures high enough to completely melt the metal and the resulting pig-iron had many impurities.

The birth of steel

The appearance of the blast-furnace in 15th century Germany heralded the birth of modern iron and steel making. The blast furnace produced much higher temperatures and consequently much purer metal.

Technological advances during the 19th century produced two new steel making processes, Bessemer's Converter (1856) and Pierre Martin's Open Hearth furnace. The present age of the motor car and countless consumer goods has created an ever growing demand for iron and steel.

Above: Haematite or Kidney ore is a very rich iron ore.

Above: Limonite or Brown ore yields only 60% iron.

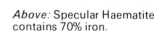

Above: Specular Haematite contains 70% iron.

Right: Ten years ago Mount Tom Price in Western Australia was virtually unknown. Today it is being torn apart by huge mechanical shovels *(above)* capable of removing over 20 tons of rock at each bite. The reason for this onslaught is iron. Over a million million tons of rich iron ore is held in the mountains of the Hamersley Range, enough to satisfy world demands for several hundred years. The ores formed many millions of years ago from iron-rich muds on the bottom of an ancient shallow sea. Once the iron-bearing rocks were lifted and exposed to weathering much of the softer mudstone was removed leaving the mountain very rich in iron.

Above: An aerial view of a modern steelworks at Corby, England. Large amounts of money, labour and land are required to build and operate large-scale steel-making plants.

Below: Because of its strength and durability steel is the most important metal used today. It has a vast number of uses, from girders to frying pans. A selection of uses is shown below.

1. The converter is charged with molten iron

Above: marine castings made in special steel.

Above: A steel tank wagon for petroleum.

Above: Some domestic steel products.

2. Oxygen and air are blown through the converter

1. In 1856 Henry Bessemer, an Englishman, proposed a method of converting iron into steel by blowing air through molten pig-iron. With few refinements Bessemer's process remains today the most important steel-making process. In the first stage of the process the furnace, shaped like a huge cement-mixer, is tipped onto its side and "charged" with up to 30 tons of molten pig-iron.

2. The charged converter is then tipped into the upright position and a blast of pre-heated air and oxygen is forced up through holes in the base. After a few minutes the temperature rises to over 1,500°C and a white flame, up to 30 feet (nine metres) long, roars from the furnace as carbon is removed from the molten metal. The whole conversion takes about 20 minutes.

3. After the "blow" the molten steel is poured into a huge ladle and a manganese alloy is added to combine with, and remove, iron oxide. The mass of steel is then either transferred into smaller ladles which are used for pouring the metal into moulds or cast directly into ingots for forging.

4. In the rolling mill ingot steel, maintained at high temperature, passes through a series of rollers which squeeze and shape the soft metal into sheets or bars of a variety of cross-sections.

3. The molten steel is poured into moulds

4. The red-hot iron is rolled into sheets

31

The story of coal

The formation of coal

Above: Plant life in the Carboniferous period (345 to 280 million years ago) was dominated by giant ferns and club-mosses.

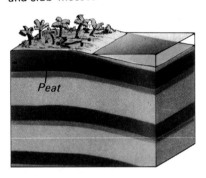

Above: Dead and decaying plant matter gradually accumulated to form vast thicknesses of peat.

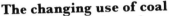

Above: Millions of years after burial the peat was transformed, by heat and pressure, into seams of coal.

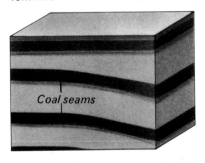

Above: This fragment of coal contains the fossilized imprint of the scales of a fish which lived in the Carboniferous period.

Earth's fossilized energy store

Millions of years ago vast areas of Europe, North America and Asia were covered by dense swampy forest. As the trees died they accumulated as thick deposits of peaty debris, clogging the waters of the swamp and gradually undergoing chemical changes. The acid swamp waters prevented the normal decomposition of plant matter by the action of bacteria and instead preserved the partially decayed carbon-rich material. Millions of years passed and these deposits gradually became buried under thousands of feet of rock. Pressure and heat forced out the remaining hydrogen and oxygen in the form of water and carbon dioxide leaving behind a high concentration of organic carbon. Further pressure completed the transformation into coal.

The changing use of coal

For 300 years coal was the most important fuel at man's disposal. It was the prime source of energy throughout the Industrial Revolution and provided the vital link between the wood-burning Middle Ages and the highly industrialized 20th century. Oil and natural gas have now taken its place as the most important sources of industrial energy and natural gas has largely replaced "town gas" which was obtained from coal.

Today, coal is widely used as a valuable raw material in the chemical industries. Plastics, fertilizers, road-building materials and even perfumes may be made from the hydrocarbon compounds extracted from coal.

Competition from other fuels has forced the coal industry into intensive research in many fields. Techniques are being developed to get the best return from coal as a fuel and as a source of raw materials.

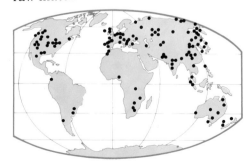

Above: The major coal-producing regions of the world.

Above: Working conditions in 19th century mines were very harsh. Women and children carried baskets of coal cut from the coal face by the miners. This print is from the Mining Report of 1842.

Above: In modern coal mines heavy duty trepanning machines tear coal from the face and feed it straight onto conveyors running back to the lift shafts. The rate of production is greatly increased by such machines.

Above: At the end of their shift miners are hoisted to the surface in powerful lifts. The safety lamp and protective helmet are vital pieces of equipment as even today mining can be a hazardous occupation.

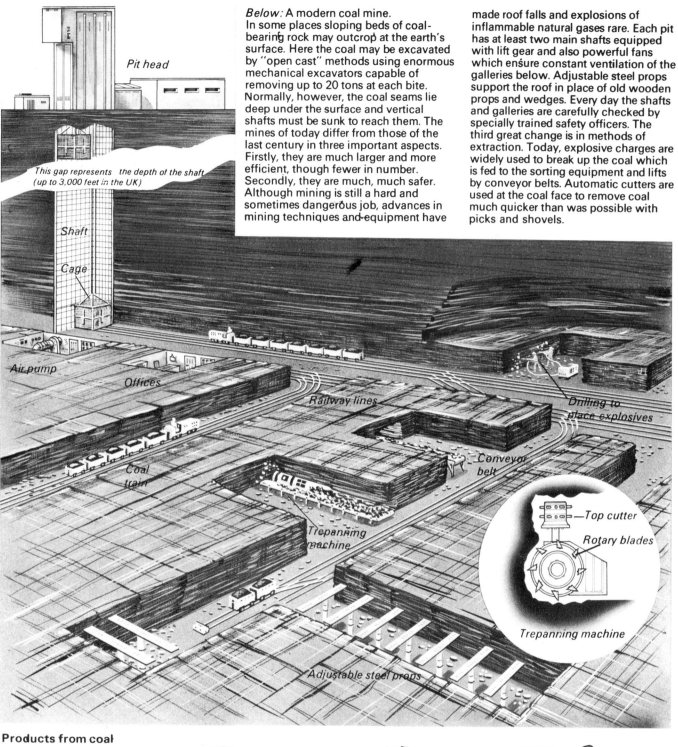

Pit head

This gap represents the depth of the shaft
(up to 3,000 feet in the UK)

Shaft

Cage

Air pump

Offices

Railway lines

Coal train

Trepanning machine

Drilling to place explosives

Conveyor belt

Top cutter

Rotary blades

Trepanning machine

Adjustable steel props

Below: A modern coal mine.
In some places sloping beds of coal-bearing rock may outcrop at the earth's surface. Here the coal may be excavated by "open cast" methods using enormous mechanical excavators capable of removing up to 20 tons at each bite. Normally, however, the coal seams lie deep under the surface and vertical shafts must be sunk to reach them. The mines of today differ from those of the last century in three important aspects. Firstly, they are much larger and more efficient, though fewer in number. Secondly, they are much, much safer. Although mining is still a hard and sometimes dangerous job, advances in mining techniques and equipment have made roof falls and explosions of inflammable natural gases rare. Each pit has at least two main shafts equipped with lift gear and also powerful fans which ensure constant ventilation of the galleries below. Adjustable steel props support the roof in place of old wooden props and wedges. Every day the shafts and galleries are carefully checked by specially trained safety officers. The third great change is in methods of extraction. Today, explosive charges are widely used to break up the coal which is fed to the sorting equipment and lifts by conveyor belts. Automatic cutters are used at the coal face to remove coal much quicker than was possible with picks and shovels.

Products from coal

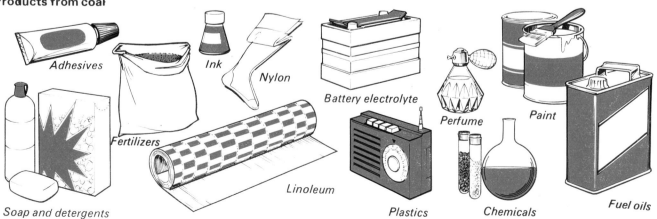

Adhesives

Ink

Nylon

Fertilizers

Battery electrolyte

Perfume

Paint

Soap and detergents

Linoleum

Plastics

Chemicals

Fuel oils

Drilling for fuel gas and oil

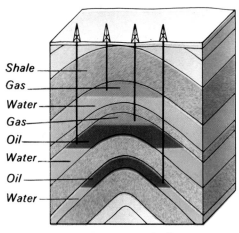

The formation of gas and oil

Above: Oil traps. The most common type of oil trap is the anticline, a geological structure in which the rocks are forced into an arch. Oil may collect in porous rock such as sandstone and is prevented from escaping by a cap-rock such as shale. Natural gas is often found in the same formation.

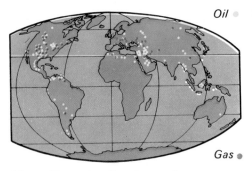

Above: The major oil and natural gas producing areas of the world.

Black gold

Oil deposits are formed in a manner similar to coal—by the deep burial, decay and compression of plants rich in carbon. The oil does not exist as reservoirs of liquid but as tiny droplets dispersed through the spaces of a porous rock such as sandstone. This rock must be covered by a cap of rock such as shale to stop the oil escaping.

When a hole is bored through the overlying strata a "gusher" of oil is forced violently upwards by the pressure in the surrounding rock. As soon as the well blows, the head is sealed off by a complex system of valves and the drilling derrick removed for use at another site.

Refining

The crude oil taken direct from the well is a sticky, heavy, dark brown or black liquid which must be refined before it will yield its wealth of raw materials. Impurities are removed and the resulting liquids, heavy fuel oils, diesel, petrol, kerosene and a host of others are piped to tankers or to further refining processes. Oil provides industry with a very important source of raw materials.

Natural gas

Natural gas, once burnt off at the well-head as a waste product, is now valued as yet another fossil fuel. The gas is easily liquefied for transport by tanker or, as in Europe, a wide area may be served by a pipeline grid.

Above: Drilling engineers at work checking the turntable of one of the permanent North Sea gas drilling rigs. This well in the Leman gas field began production in 1968.
Left: In 1859 Edwin L. Drake struck oil in Oil Creek, Pennsylvania, and unwittingly sparked off one of the greatest booms in American history. By 1860 the whole of Oil Creek Valley, a tributary of the Allegheny River, was leased or purchased by prospectors. The entire valley had become a forest of drilling towers with over 70 wells producing 1,200 barrels of oil a day. By 1864 production had risen to over 6,000 barrels a day. The wasteful competition of dozens of individual wells on the same oil field continued until well into the 1930s when some of the larger owners began to buy out the small operators. Today, large companies produce most of the oil and gas as it is a very expensive business.

Above: A pipeline bringing oil from Fahud in the Oman to the coast where it will be put on a tanker.

Above: The giant tanker *Esso Ulidia* is one of the new breed of super-tankers.

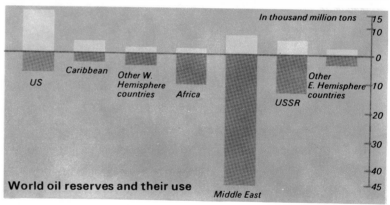

In thousand million tons

US Caribbean Other W. Hemisphere countries Africa USSR Other E. Hemisphere countries

Middle East

World oil reserves and their use

A drilling rig

Drill derrick

Engine house

Rotary table

Mud pump

Drilling bit

Above centre: To be efficient, oil refineries must operate 24 hours a day. The photograph shows Fawley refinery, near Southampton, England, at night.
Above: World oil reserves compared with total output over the years. The blue columns give the amount of oil already mined in that area. The dark green columns underneath show how much oil is left in reserve. If no new oilfields are found it is possible that all the oil reserves could be used up by 1989. The Middle East countries are by far the biggest producers of oil.
Left: The main parts of an oil-drilling rig. The diamond drilling bit is connected to the rig by lengths of rigid steel pipe. In hard rock, drilling a 10,000 foot (3,048 metres) hole can take 90 days.
Right: A permanent platform for obtaining gas from under the North Sea. Sited at the Leman gas field it began production in 1968.

Minerals for modern technology

Creation of nuclear fission

1. Neutron fired at nucleus

2. Becomes unstable

3. Nucleus is ripped apart

4. Energy is released

Above: Nuclear fission occurs when an atomic nucleus "captures" a stray neutron, becomes unstable and breaks up, releasing a vast amount of energy in a minute fraction of a second.

Creation of nuclear fusion

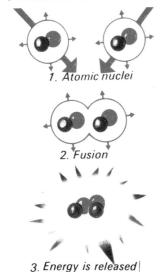

1. Atomic nuclei

2. Fusion

3. Energy is released

Above: Fusion, or thermonuclear reactions, occur when two light atomic nuclei combine and release energy. The fusion of hydrogen nuclei, the sun's major source of energy, may also provide man with a future source of energy. In the past, dangerous radioactive waste has been encased in lead and concrete and either buried or dumped at sea. Natural salt deposits act as effective radiation shields and may be an answer to nuclear waste disposal problems (*right*).

A fast breeder reactor

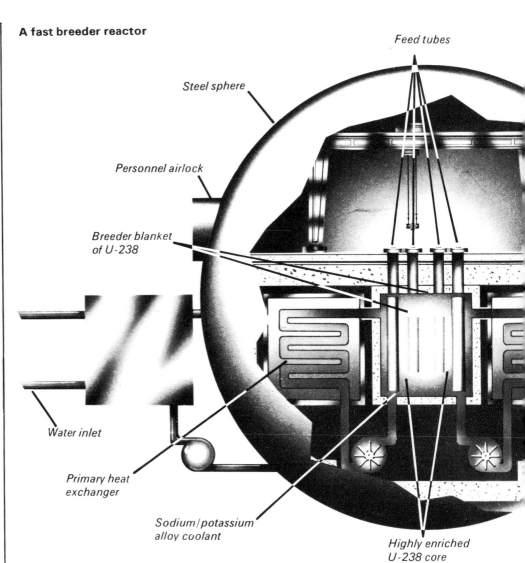

- Steel sphere
- Feed tubes
- Personnel airlock
- Breeder blanket of U-238
- Water inlet
- Primary heat exchanger
- Sodium/potassium alloy coolant
- Highly enriched U-238 core

A possible way of disposing of nuclear waste

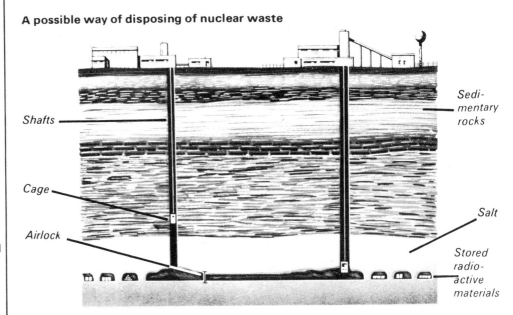

- Shafts
- Cage
- Airlock
- Sedimentary rocks
- Salt
- Stored radioactive materials

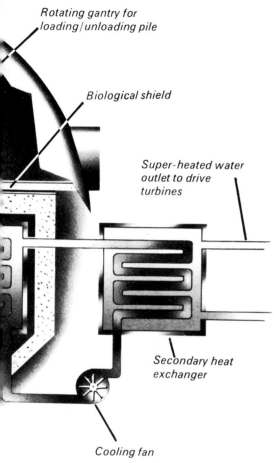

Rotating gantry for
loading/unloading pile

Biological shield

Super-heated water
outlet to drive
turbines

Secondary heat
exchanger

Cooling fan

Specialist materials

The rapid growth of science and technology over the past 20 years has led to a constant and ever increasing demand for new and specialist materials. The resources of the earth are being used as never before. As supplies of traditional fossil fuels, oil, coal and gas become exhausted man looks for new sources of power. Nuclear energy from radioactive minerals such as uranium will become more and more important. Minerals are being used to create new materials such as plastics. Chemistry has developed the range of materials which we now use.

New techniques

In every industry new techniques are being developed to use both old and new materials. The demands of the 20th century have led man to investigate new areas of knowledge. The laser, which has at its heart a ruby, was once an interesting experimental device. Today it is being used in delicate surgical operations; as a carrier of telephone messages and in industry as a cutting tool. The computer which relies on a vast selection of special materials has become part of modern life.

A simple ruby laser

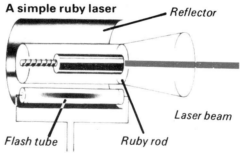

Reflector

Laser beam

Flash tube   Ruby rod

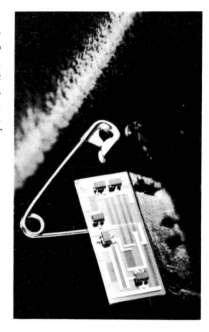

Above: Microcircuits are one of the technological wonders of the 20th century. By adding impurities to a single chip of pure silicon crystal, different parts of the crystal may be given different electrical properties. Just one of these minute integrated circuits, a tenth of an inch square and a few thousandths of an inch thick, may contain scores of "components".
Left: The laser is a beam of light amplified to many times its normal energy level. Inside a simple laser there is a source of light, something like a neon light, which is flashed on and off very quickly. This light is reflected on to a ruby crystal which organizes the light in a very powerful beam. The beam is powerful enough to burn through steel yet accurate enough to be used in delicate surgery.
Below: A laser beam being used in medical research.

Above: Power for the future will almost certainly rely more and more on nuclear fuels as the traditional fossil fuel supplies are exhausted. In the "pile" of the fast breeder reactor, raw fast neutrons are used to bombard specially prepared uranium fuel rods and maintain the chain reaction. The reaction generates tremendous heat which is passed through heat exchangers to produce steam for the turbines. The turbines then generate electricity.

The new breed of "fast" reactors based on plutonium fuel can not only generate an enormous amount of heat from a small amount of fuel but can create their own fuel faster than the original is used up. In the future, energy supplies may be based on reactors using fuel extracted from naturally occurring granite.

Nuclear power stations are an efficient way of generating power but they are expensive to build and run. It is hoped that these costs will be reduced and we will have a cheap and easy power source. In countries which have few natural fuels such as coal or oil, nuclear power should be especially valuable.

Ceramics and glass

Above: A kaolin mine near St. Austell, Cornwall, England. It is one of the largest kaolin mines in Europe. Kaolin is a clay found in various parts of the world. Pure kaolin is white and remains white when heated. The finest china ware is made from pure kaolin. Less pure kaolin is used to make a vast variety of other ceramic products.

Right: A potter's wheel in use. Pottery can be shaped by hand but the wheel, invented about 5,000 years ago, makes a much better product. Shaping clay on a revolving wheel is called *throwing.*

After an object has been shaped it must be treated to make it keep its shape. The first process it goes through is *drying.* Water in the clay is made to evaporate by slowly passing it through a warm tunnel. When this stage is complete, the pottery is hard enough to pick up but not durable enough for use.

Right: A pottery kiln. To make pottery very hard it must be heated in a very hot oven called a kiln. This process is called *firing.* Very high temperatures, 1,200–1,500°C, are needed for high quality ceramics such as porcelain. Coarse pottery requires much lower temperatures.

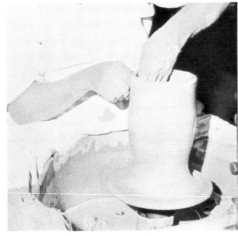

Clues to the past

Ceramics, the making of wares from clay, is one of man's oldest industries. All types of clay ware, from bricks to china, are included in the term ceramics which comes from the Greek word for a potter. Primitive man of about 25,000 years ago was probably the first to make things out of clay. All cultures have made ceramics but the Egyptians are believed to have been the first to make good quality pottery. They were using the potter's wheel around 2,500 BC and knew how to glaze and fire pottery. Much of what is known about vanished civilizations has been learnt from careful study of ancient pottery.

The modern world has found ceramics to be essential and versatile products. Not only are they used in their traditional form as domestic ware but in countless industrial applications from steel-making to spaceships.

An ancient craft

Glassmaking is also an ancient industry but not as old as ceramics. Five thousand years ago the Egyptians were making glass for beads and ornaments. Their techniques were acquired by other Mediterranean countries and the manufacture of glass gradually spread. It is made by heating soda, lime and sand. When the first atomic bomb was exploded in the New Mexico desert in 1945, a vast area was turned into a sheet of glass.

Today it is mass-produced in vast quantities to make bottles, windows and innumerable other products.

Most ceramics used in the home are called whiteware and can include everything from plates, cups and dishes to glazed tiles for walls and floors.

The ability of ceramics to resist chemical attack makes them ideal for use as sinks, bathroom fittings, roofing tiles and as pipes for sewerage and drainage.

Industrial ceramics withstand very high temperatures. They are essential in steel making and are used in space capsules *(above)* to shield them when entering the atmosphere.

Electrical porcelain makes an excellent insulator and is found in all kinds of electrical equipment, such as that seen above, and in the ordinary light-bulb socket.

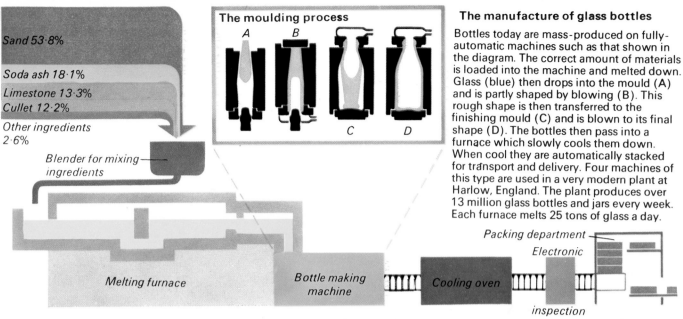

Sand 53·8%

Soda ash 18·1%

Limestone 13·3%

Cullet 12·2%

Other ingredients 2·6%

Blender for mixing ingredients

The moulding process

A   B

C   D

Melting furnace

Bottle making machine

Cooling oven

Packing department

Electronic inspection

The manufacture of glass bottles

Bottles today are mass-produced on fully-automatic machines such as that shown in the diagram. The correct amount of materials is loaded into the machine and melted down. Glass (blue) then drops into the mould (A) and is partly shaped by blowing (B). This rough shape is then transferred to the finishing mould (C) and is blown to its final shape (D). The bottles then pass into a furnace which slowly cools them down. When cool they are automatically stacked for transport and delivery. Four machines of this type are used in a very modern plant at Harlow, England. The plant produces over 13 million glass bottles and jars every week. Each furnace melts 25 tons of glass a day.

Left: Highly polished sheet glass for use in windows can now be mass-produced by floating molten glass on a bath of molten tin. Molten tin is perfectly flat and smooth and so the floating glass spreads into an absolutely flat sheet. When cool, the sheet is highly polished on both sides and needs no further processing as did older methods.
Right: A coffee jar about to be moulded into shape.
Bottom right: The traditional method of shaping glass is by blowing. It calls for skill and timing as the molten glass used is cooling all the time. First, the end of a long metal blowpipe is dipped into a tank of molten glass. The thick, runny mass is then rolled on a smooth iron table so that there is an equal amount around the end of the pipe. The *blower* then blows a bubble, all the time turning the pipe to prevent the glass from drooping under its own weight. Once he has a big enough bubble, it can be opened up and shaped with hand tools. Moulds are also used to form the molten glass into the correct shape.

The finest quality glass, called cut glass. It has been prized for centuries for its clarity and its ability to be shaped into elegant ornaments, glasses and vases.

Pyrosil is an immensely strong glass which is able to withstand sharp temperature changes without cracking. It is used in the home as it can be put over a naked flame.

A special glass called Triplex is used for windshields as it does not shatter. Here a windshield for a locomotive has been tested by firing a stone at it.

Scientific glassware for laboratory work is required in a large variety of shapes and sizes. Modern technology has made it possible to mass-produce such objects.

Products of the earth in everyday life

New materials

The 20th century has seen a revolution in the building industry throughout the world. Every year countless new materials are developed by the metal and chemical industries for their strength, lightness, versatility and cheapness. Many of these materials were unheard of 20 years ago. Whereas the buildings of the Middle Ages were largely of wood and plaster and those of the last few centuries of stone and brick, we are now in the age of concrete and glass, steel and plastics.

Man-made materials

Each year more natural materials are replaced by man-made alternatives, many of which are not only stronger and cheaper but also damp- and fire-proof. Already, glass and plastics can be made with the strength of steel and windows may be made to darken automatically in bright sunlight. The 200 storey buildings and plastic domed cities of the science writer may not be very far away.

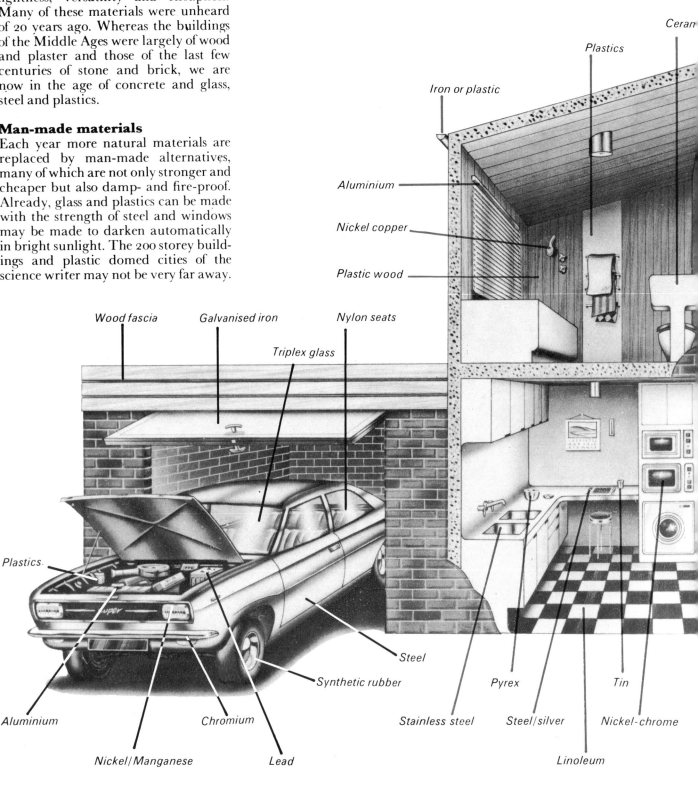

Merc

Ceram

Plastics

Iron or plastic

Aluminium

Nickel copper

Plastic wood

Wood fascia

Galvanised iron

Nylon seats

Triplex glass

Plastics

Aluminium

Nickel/Manganese

Chromium

Lead

Steel

Synthetic rubber

Stainless steel

Pyrex

Steel/silver

Linoleum

Tin

Nickel-chrome

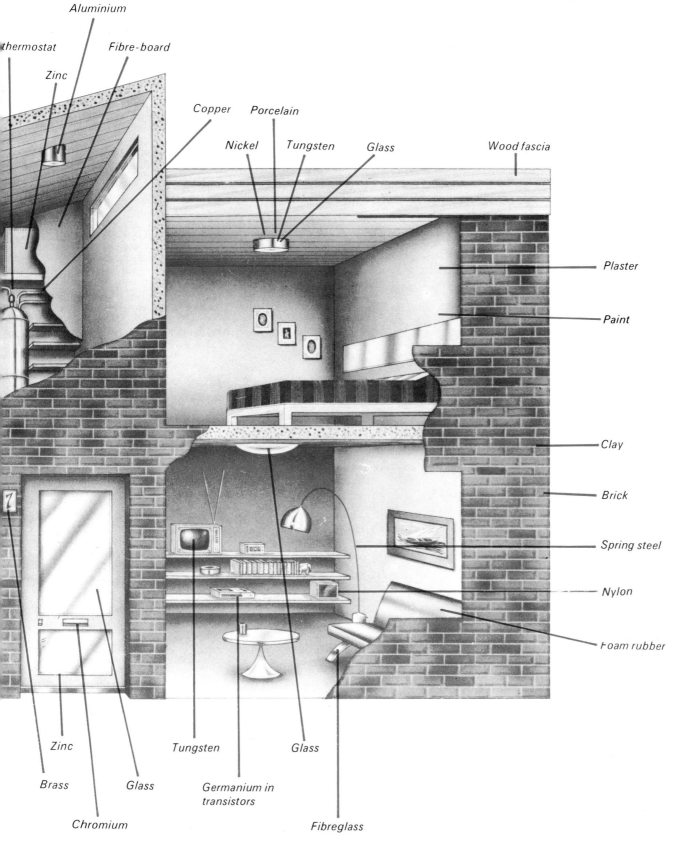

Aluminium

thermostat

Fibre-board

Zinc

Copper

Porcelain

Nickel

Tungsten

Glass

Wood fascia

Plaster

Paint

Clay

Brick

Spring steel

Nylon

Foam rubber

Zinc

Tungsten

Glass

Brass

Glass

Germanium in transistors

Chromium

Fibreglass

41

The future man and the earth

Above: The Colorado River, Mexico, laden with silt, amply illustrates the rate at which natural forces of erosion are wearing away the continents.

Right: Estimates of the amounts of rocks and minerals removed and created every year. In the last few hundred years man has probably helped to double the rate of erosion. Even this does not allow for his annual "take" of 15,000 million tons per year of metals, fuels etc.

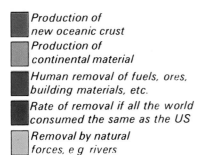

■ *Production of new oceanic crust*
■ *Production of continental material*
■ *Human removal of fuels, ores, building materials, etc.*
■ *Rate of removal if all the world consumed the same as the US*
□ *Removal by natural forces, e g rivers*

Right: The graph shows the estimated life span of some of the world's metals based on population growth and increasing demand for goods. Even allowing for the discovery of new mineral deposits, it is likely that man may soon face a severe world shortage of metals. Metals such as lead, zinc, tin and gold could all be used by 1990. Others such as manganese, nickel and copper may last beyond 2,100 but the costs of mining them will greatly increase. The earth is not inexhaustible. Man is now taking metals from the earth far more quickly than they can be replaced by natural processes. Two alternatives are possible. One is to ensure that waste is eliminated and that materials are reused. The other is to look at the oceans, the last great reserve of earth's mineral wealth. Reclaiming minerals from the sea and sea bed will be costly but vitally important to mankind.

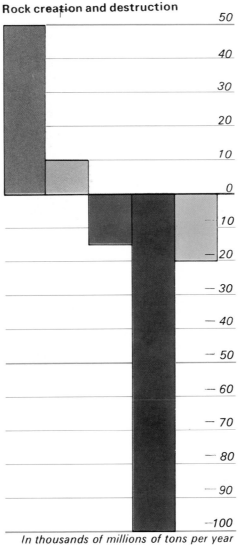

Rock creation and destruction

50
40
30
20
10
0
—10
—20
— 30
— 40
— 50
— 60
— 70
— 80
— 90
—100

In thousands of millions of tons per year

Man changes the earth

Never before in the 600 million year history of life on earth has one species held the position of power held by man today. Other species have dominated the earth, the dinosaurs did for 100 million years, but man is the only one to develop the power to completely change his environment at will.

The present population of 3,600 million is predicted to soar to 7,000 million by the year 2000. Every year man takes more from the earth—minerals, water, rock, food resources of every kind. Every year more and more waste is pumped back into our rivers and oceans, poisoning them and the life in them. Much of our wildlife is in great danger of extinction and the cities continue to spread into the countryside.

Diminishing resources

The answers to these urgent problems lie within man's reach. The resources of our planet will not last for ever. They must be conserved and used wisely just as the farmer looks after his fields to avoid exhausting them. Raw materials must be re-cycled and re-used, not heedlessly thrown away. The animal and plant life of this planet must be protected against the destructive effects of rapid industrialization.

If man will learn from past errors he can and must do all in his power to avoid destroying the planet which gave him life.

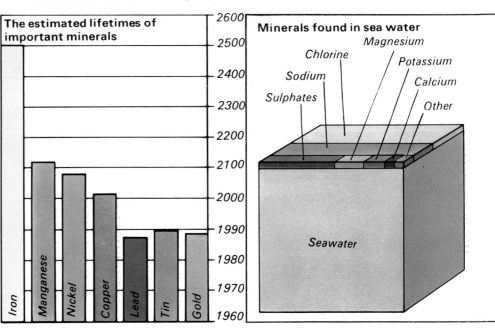

The estimated lifetimes of important minerals

2600
2500
2400
2300
2200
2100
2000
1990
1980
1970
1960

Iron · Manganese · Nickel · Copper · Lead · Tin · Gold

Minerals found in sea water

Magnesium
Chlorine
Potassium
Sodium
Calcium
Sulphates
Other

Seawater

Left: One of the major problems in an over-crowded, consumer-orientated world is what to do with waste. Recent public outcry at the increasing number of hideous dumping grounds has led technologists to consider ways of re-using waste materials.
Above: Cars, once left to rust in ugly car-cemeteries, are now fed into giant machines which shred the metal before returning it to the steelworks for re-use.

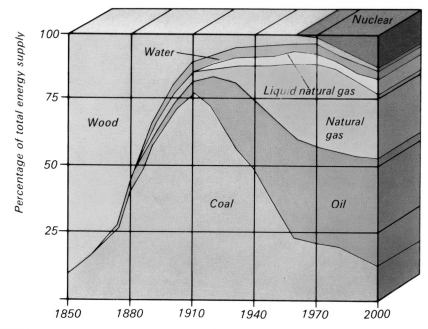

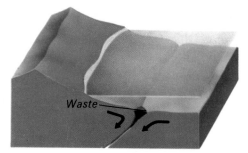

Above: The ultimate dustbin. It has been suggested that man might be able to use his recently acquired knowledge of crustal plates to solve his growing problem of municipal and industrial waste disposal. If dumped over a descending current, particularly in a region of rapid sedimentation, waste would disappear forever in the interior of the earth.
Left: The rapidly changing sources of energy in the US are shown in the graph. As the fossil fuels decline towards the end of the century nuclear power continues to grow in importance.

Left: One cubic mile of sea-water contains up to 170 million tons of dissolved minerals. The diagram shows the major constituents of sea-water. At present only common salt, manganese and bromine are commercially extracted from sea-water. In the future much of man's copper, cobalt, zinc and nickel may have to be won from the sea.
Right: Manganese extracted from sea-water at a plant on the Gulf of Mexico.
Far right: The sea-bed is also a source of minerals. Sulphur is known to exist in large quantities in the rock of salt domes buried beneath the ocean beds. The mineral can be extracted by pumping superheated water into the deposit and extracting the sulphur from the liquid.

Projects find out more about the earth

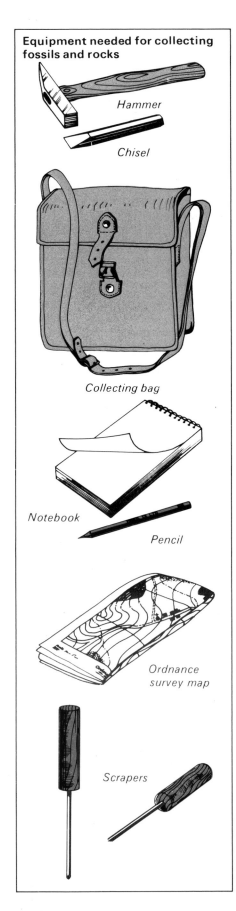

Equipment needed for collecting fossils and rocks

Hammer

Chisel

Collecting bag

Notebook

Pencil

Ordnance survey map

Scrapers

Starting a rock and mineral collection

The best way to learn about minerals and rocks is to collect them. It requires no special equipment and can be carried out almost everywhere. The items shown on the left are the basic tools of the specimen collector. A geologist's hammer and a cold chisel are needed to chip away pieces of rock. A large strong bag is necessary for carrying the tools and specimens. As it is essential to note where the specimens were found a notebook and pencil are vital. A map of the area, preferably a geological map, is a very useful aid. Scrapers made from large nails are useful for cleaning specimens.

The best places to find specimens are where rocks have been uncovered by natural forces—river banks, cliffs, etc. Quarries, railway cuttings and tunnels are also fruitful sites but permission should be asked for first.

At home, specimens must be stored in a careful way. The ideal thing is a cabinet with drawers divided into sections but this is not essential. Cardboard boxes divided in a similar way are enough for beginning a collection.

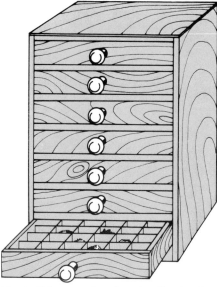

The building up of a mineral collection is an interesting hobby but it is much more fun to try to identify what they are. You need a really good reference book on minerals for this, preferably one with colour illustrations.

Simple tests can be carried out to try to identify minerals oneself. Given below are some of the easier tests. More complicated tests can be attempted if you become very interested in the subject. These can be found in any reference book.

To get experience in identifying minerals it is worth going along to a local museum which has a geological collection. A careful study of the exhibits will give a good idea of the variety of rocks and minerals and what they look like.

Lustre

Many rocks are dull and ordinary looking. Others may have a shiny or glistening appearance, which can be generally described as *lustre*. The kind of lustre they exhibit can often be a guide as to their composition. *Metallic* lustre exhibits the shininess of metals—a common feature of certain metallic ores. Where the shine is more dull, but still metallic, this is called *submetallic* lustre. *Vitreous* lustre means the shininess of glass—like the surface of a newly fractured flint, for example. Again, if not so shiny but still 'glassy' it can be called *subvitreous*. Silky means a silk-like lustre—a typical characteristic of minerals which have a fibrous structure, like satin-spar and varieties of asbestos. *Resinous* means the lustre of resin—like opal or amber, for example. *Pearly* means an opalescent lustre. *Adamantine* means a brilliant lustre like that of a diamond.

These are the main types of lustre, and they are easy enough to remember. They are more useful than colour as a description of a particular mineral. But remember that the true lustre will only show up on freshly broken faces of specimens. Use a geologist's hammer to break open specimens for examination.

Streak

This is another simple test which can often be useful in identifying minerals. Rubbed over a harder surface, some specimens will leave a coloured mark or streak. In the case of soft rocks, the specimen can be rubbed over the surface of a porcelain tile (or even a piece of stout paper) to see if it forms a streak. With harder minerals, it will be necessary to rub the specimen over a file.

The colour of the streak is not always helpful, though. In many cases, regardless of the colour of the specimen, the streak will be white. But there are the exceptions which can provide a very strong clue as regards identification.

The best are those where the colour of the streak is very different to the colour of the specimen itself. Here there are two outstanding common examples:
HEMATITE which is black, gives a red streak.
PYRITES which is brassy yellow, gives a green or brownish-black streak.

Not quite so good are the minerals which give a streak of similar colour to that of the specimen, but either definitely lighter or darker. For example, MALACHITE, which is bright green, gives a paler green streak: and RUTILE, which is red-brown, gives a pale brown streak. CALCITE gives a white streak. The mineral is colourless or white, sometimes with grey, yellow, blue, red, brown or black tints.

Hardness

One of the ways of classifying rocks and minerals is by their hardness, and this can also be helpful for identification. A harder substance will always mark or scratch a softer one, which is the basis of a simple test for hardness—see Moh's Hardness Scale.

Appearance is no guide to hardness. For example, Serpentine, a varied coloured rock, looks and feels "solid" enough, but it is actually fairly soft (hardness 3-4). It can easily be cut and carved with a knife or wood chisel (hardness about 6-6.5).

Moh's Hardness Scale

On Moh's Scale—which is a standard reference for mineralogists—the hardness of minerals is defined by numbers, starting with 1 for very soft (i.e. Talc) up to 10 for the hardest mineral known (Diamond).

It is quite easy to establish the hardness of any mineral, and this can be done on the spot using the simple references shown. For example, any specimen which can be scratched by a thumb nail has a hardness of 2 or less; anything scratched by a copper coin or an iron nail a hardness of 3 or less; and so on.

This also works the other way. Thus if a specimen scratches a copper coin it will have a hardness of more than 3.5; and if it scratches a piece of glass, a hardness of more than 4.5. Then if it can be scratched by a penknife, its hardness will obviously lie between 4.5 and 6.5.

Using this simple technique you should be able to establish the hardness of any unknown mineral fairly accurately. You are unlikely to find any minerals in the hardness range much above 7, so a piece of flint is the hardest "test piece" you are likely to require. Check that it does have a hardness of about 7 (it should scratch a knife, but can be marked with a file).

Moh's Hardness Scale	
1. Talc	
2. Rock salt	
	2.5 Thumb nail
3. Calcspar	
	3.5 Copper coin or iron nail
4. Fluorspar	
	4.5-5 Piece of glass
5. Apatite	
6. Feldspar	
	6.5 Penknife
7. Quartz, flint	
	7.5 File
8. Topaz	
9. Sapphire	
10. Diamond	

Collecting fossils

When rock collecting always be on the lookout for fossils. The same equipment is needed and it can lead to a fascinating study of the earth's long and exciting past. Indeed you may find that fossil collecting interests you more than rock and mineral collecting.

Fossil collecting is an art which improves with practice. Don't be disappointed if you fail to find spectacular samples at the first attempt. You will soon develop the knack of looking in the right places. Most fossils are found in sedimentary rocks, so cliffs, river banks and other natural rock exposures are the best places to look. Quarries, road and railway cuttings are also good places but extreme care must be taken and permission always obtained.

Maps are an essential aid for the fossil collector. They can help you to find where sedimentary rocks are and so make your search easier. There are many books on fossils which will give you information on the types of fossils and their ages. It is worth buying a simple book first.

Finding and preparing fossils

Take time to survey the area. Look for rock surfaces which have been exposed by the weather. Some fossils may be immediately seen but most are to be found inside rocks. Rocks should be carefully cracked open with a hammer. If a fossil is discovered, chip away most of the rock around it and leave further cleaning and preparation until you get home. The place where you found the fossil should be noted and a number put on the fossil for identification.

Cleaning can be done with a fine chisel or scrapers made from nails as shown (*below left*). Delicate specimens may be improved and protected by a thin coat of clear varnish.

Identification of fossils

There is an enormous variety of fossils but careful study of the types can give the beginner a rough idea of what he has found. A study of living plants and animals is also very helpful in understanding fossils. Some fossil types died out millions of years ago but others have present-day relations in living plants. A good collection of fossils will give an idea of how life on earth has changed and the vast periods of time involved.

If you cannot identify a fossil it is worth visiting a local museum which has displays of fossils. Most large towns and cities have such displays, usually of the local area and you will find specimens carefully laid out there. If you think that you have an unusual fossil it is worth asking to see the curator of the museum. He may identify it as a rare specimen.

Museums and exhibits of fossils

The list below is a selection of some of the museums which have exhibits of fossils:
British Museum (Natural History), London
Royal Scottish Museum, Edinburgh
National Museum of Wales, Cardiff
Scarborough Museum, Yorkshire
Sedgewick Museum, Cambridge
The University Museum, Oxford
Exeter Museum
Ipswich Museum

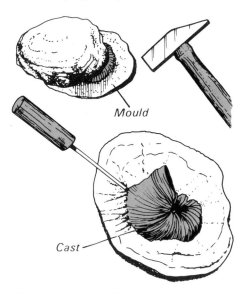

Mould

Cast

Revealing a fossil

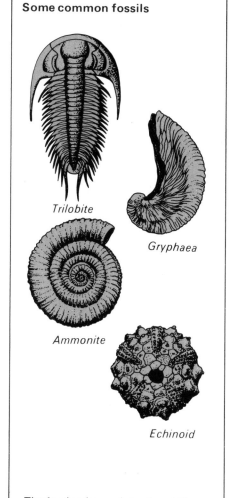

Trilobite

Gryphaea

Ammonite

Echinoid

Some common fossils

The fascinating variety of past life forms makes fossil collecting one of the most rewarding of all collecting hobbies. Some forms such as the trilobite *(Top left)* vanished millions of years ago whilst others such as the Jurassic echinoid *(Bottom right)* have a wide range of present day relatives.

Grow your own crystals

Right: Place two dessertspoons of potash alum, available from any chemist, into a jam jar of water and warm up the mixture in a pan until the crystals are dissolved. Pour the hot solution into a clean jar, stopper tightly and leave to cool. Sprinkle a few crystals of alum into the cold solution. This will leave a "saturated" solution. Pour a little of this liquid into a shallow dish, cover and leave to evaporate dry. Then choose one small well-shaped crystal and suspend it in the jar of solution. With care and patience beautiful crystals may be grown.

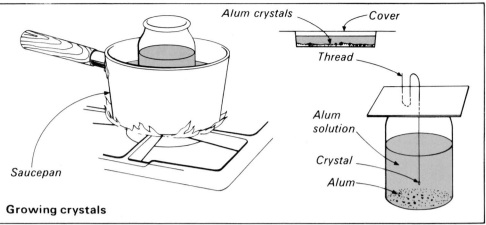

Growing crystals

Finding out about soil

Taking a sample of soil

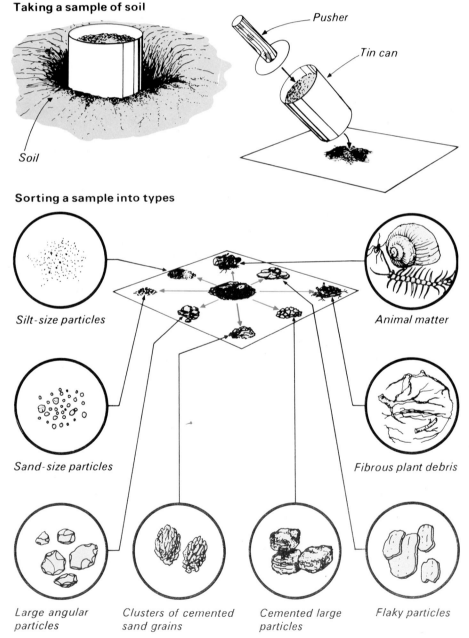

Soil

Pusher

Tin can

Sorting a sample into types

Silt-size particles

Animal matter

Sand-size particles

Fibrous plant debris

Large angular particles

Clusters of cemented sand grains

Cemented large particles

Flaky particles

What is soil?

Cut both ends carefully from an ordinary domestic can and nail one of the ends to a wooden handle. Press the open cylinder into the soil until flush with the surface, tilt slightly and lift out carefully. This is easier in damp soil. Weigh a clean, dry plate and then use the "pusher" to force all the soil sample out on to the plate and weigh again. Subtract to obtain the sample weight. Using a magnifying glass and a piece of wire or fine screwdriver, sort the sample into piles of angular grains, round grains, clusters of cemented grains, fibres of plant matter and any other notable categories.

Leave indoors for a day or two and weigh each pile. Do they add up to the original sample weight? If the weight of the sample has fallen it is because its moisture has evaporated. Construct a simple graph *(below)* for each of several samples taken from different areas and compare the composition of the soils. Can you explain any of the differences?

The composition of a soil sample

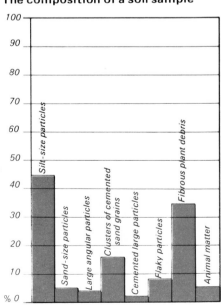

Index

Illustration Credits

Key to the positions of illustrations: (T) top, (C) centre, (B) bottom and combinations; for example (TR) top right, or (CL) centre left.

Artists

Noel Singer/Garden Studio: 3
Eric Jewell & Associates: 4—5, 6—7, 14—15, 18—19, 21 (T), 33, 35, 39
Colin Rose: 7 (BR), 8—9, 10—11, 12—13, 16—17, 20, 21 (B), 23 (CR), 29, 30, 32, 34, 42—43, 44—45, 46
David Jefferis: 22—23, 24—25, 33 (T), 36—37, 40—41

Photographs and Prints

Rob Bock/Bruce Coleman Ltd.: Front Cover (TL)
Mansell Collection: 4 (TL), 5 (BR), 21 (BL), 25, 28 (T), 28 (C), 30 (TL), 32 (TR)
Ronan Picture Library and Royal Astronomical Society: 4 (BL), 4 (BR)
John R. Freeman & Co.: 5 (BL)
British Museum: 5 (TR); Natural History: 21 (C)
Geological Museum, London, Crown Copyright: 6, 13 (BR), 20, 26—27, Front Cover (TR)
Trans-Antarctic Expedition 1955—8. Sir Vivian Fuchs: 11
Camera Press Ltd.: 13 (TR), 22, Front and Back Cover (BR)
US Information Service: 15, 17 (BR), 21 (TR)
Japanese National Tourist Organisation: 17 (TR)
Keystone Press Agency Ltd.: 17 (C)

Associated Press: 19 (T), Front Cover (BL)
Wyoming Travel Commission: 19 (B)
De Re Metallica, Basel, 1556: 28 (TL)
De Beers Diamond Co.: 28 (BC), 28 (BR), 29 (B)
Shell Petroleum Co. Ltd.: 29 (T), 35 (TL), 35 (BR)
Osborn Hadfield Steel Foundries Ltd.: 30 (BL)
Rio Tinto Zinc: 30 (BR)
Institute of Geological Sciences, London: 30 (TR)
British Steel Corporation: 31
National Coal Board: 32 (BL), 32 (CR), 32 (BR)
Texas Co.: 34 (BL)
Esso Petroleum Co. Ltd.: 34—35 (C), 35 (TR), 35 (CR)
Ferranti Ltd.: 37 (TR)
UK Atomic Energy Authority: 37 (BR)
English China Clay: 38 (T)
Wedgwood: 38 (CT), 38 (CB)
Spode Ltd.: 38 (BL)
Doulton Sanitary Potteries Ltd.: 38 (BCL)
NASA: 38 (BCR), 42
Doulton Insulators: 38 (BR)
Pilkingtons: 39 (TR)
United Glass: 39 (TR), 39 (CR)
Jobling: 39 (BCL), 39 (BR)
Triplex: 39 (BCR)
George Cohen, 600 Group Ltd.: 43 (TR & TL)
Freeport Minerals Co., New York: 43 (BR)
DOW Chemicals, US: 43 (BL)
Natural History Photographic Agency: Back Cover (BL)